GO

RUPERT SHORTT

God Is No Thing

Coherent Christianity

HURST & COMPANY, LONDON

First published in the United Kingdom in 2016 by
C. Hurst & Co. (Publishers) Ltd.,
41 Great Russell Street, London, WC1B 3PL

This paperback edition first published in the United Kingdom in 2024 by
C. Hurst & Co. (Publishers) Ltd.,
New Wing, Somerset House, Strand, London WC2R 1LA
© Rupert Shortt, 2024

Distributed in the United States, Canada and Latin America by
Oxford University Press, 198 Madison Avenue, New York, NY 10016,
United States of America.

The right of Rupert Shortt to be identified as the author of
this publication is asserted by him in accordance with the
Copyright, Designs and Patents Act, 1988.

A Cataloguing-in-Publication data record for this book
is available from the British Library.

ISBN: 9781805261612

This book is printed using paper from registered sustainable
and managed sources.

www.hurstpublishers.com

For Timothy McDermott (1926–2014) and Clare Carlisle

Everyone who loves has been born of God and knows God.

1 John 4:7

God may well be loved, but not thought. By love may he be gotten and holden; but by thought never.

The Cloud of Unknowing, Chapter 6

St Thomas's position differs from that of modern agnostics because while modern agnosticism simply says, 'We do not know, and the universe is a mysterious riddle,' a Thomist says, 'We do not know what the answer is, but we do know that there is a mystery behind it all which we do not know, and if there were not, there would not even be a riddle. This Unknown we call *God*. If there were no God, there would be no universe to be mysterious, and nobody to be mystified.'

Victor White, *God the Unknown*

Not a death for a death, but a life for a death; forgive, redeem, re-create, refuse the evil of the past, insist on the good of the future ...

Christopher Fry, Foreword to *The Dark Is Light Enough*

CONTENTS

ACKNOWLEDGEMENTS

Some of the most deeply felt words in *God Is No Thing* come at the end. I am conscious of having nothing that I have not received. For suggesting that I turn a brief essay in defence of Christianity into a more substantial text, I am grateful to my agent, Tim Bates. Great gratitude is due to Michael Dwyer of Hurst for taking up my proposal, and to his colleagues Alasdair Craig and Alison Alexanian for their unfailing attention to detail and many kindnesses thereafter. Research grants were generously awarded to me by the Porticus Trust, the John Booth Charitable Foundation, and the Society of Authors.

I am abidingly indebted to all my colleagues at the *TLS*, especially Andrew Irwin, who read a draft of the manuscript and offered a valuable atheist perspective. Many other friends have nourished my thinking over a longer period. I am most grateful to John Barton, Lucy Beckett, Jonathan Benthall, Pedro Bernal, Ken Carter, Sarah Coakley, Madeline and Joost Cohen, Richard Conrad OP, John Cottingham, Serena Cox, Alex Gath, the late Colin Gunton, Johannes Hoff, Arnold Hunt, Muhammad al-Hussaini, John Kennedy, Bernice and David Martin, Janet Martin Soskice, Gary Michalek,

ACKNOWLEDGEMENTS

Abeydin Moosuddee, Glyn Paflin, John Polkinghorne, Timothy Radcliffe OP, Christoph Schwöbel, Alison Shell, Rosa María Valverde, the late John Whale, Rowan Williams and Jenny Willis.

Rupert Shortt
London, 2016

FOG IN A CRAGGY LANDSCAPE

Christianity—at its centre, the story of love's mending of wounded hearts—forms a potent resource for making sense of our existence. It provides the strongest available underpinning for values including the sanctity of life, the dignity of the individual, and human responsibility for the environment. It is the only world faith apart from Judaism to have weathered the storms of modernity. The state of contemporary academic philosophy is such that many of life's big questions are being better addressed by theology. For all their shortcomings, the Churches are the greatest single fount of social capital on earth. Say these things with confidence in many quarters, however (especially among intellectuals and opinion formers), and you are likely to prompt scepticism or outright scorn.

This book springs from two core convictions. One is that agnosticism and atheism are reasonable worldviews. If you are in two minds about religion or sure that you reject it, then you should naturally be true to yourself. Christians who question this may need reminding that loving your neighbour partly entails having respect for his or her opinions. The other is that Christianity gets dismissed too readily in the West today. The mockers and doubters are well advised to take a fresh look at the case for the defence, or at least to become better informed about what they are saying no to.

Any claim about the sidelining of faith will draw a swift protest from some. Public religious voices in North America and parts of Europe are often robust and some-times shrill. In the UK, of course, Church and State are still officially connected, even if the cords that bind them have been slackening for over 150 years. Perhaps it is precisely these factors which render dislike of Christianity among religion's *bien-pensant* critics all the more pointed. A few random examples confirm a broader pattern. In the supposedly subversive minstrels' gallery of our cul-ture, 'rebellion' can be no more than trite orthodoxy. The comedian Frank Skinner, who returned to the Church a few years ago, has quipped that to succeed in his trade, you need to 'wear skinny jeans, have hair like a chrysanthemum, and be an atheist'.[1] In a BBC inter-view, the painter and printmaker Anthony Green declared that a focus on religious themes can be the kiss of death to an artist's career.[2] Discussing Marilynne Robinson's acclaimed novels *Gilead*, *Home* and *Lila*, the journalist Bryan Appleyard has written that these works will seem curious to a large number of readers, 'because what is going on here is religion'.[3] He went on to argue that 'many, probably most, British people—artists, writers, audiences—will find this exotic because to them, religion has been embarrassed out of existence.' Brian Cox's high reputations as a physicist and broadcaster are secure. But in suggesting an equivalence between reflecting on the existence of God and that of witches,[4] he strayed well beyond his spheres of competence. Robinson stands out as a considerable Christian thinker, as well as a novelist. By contrast, an ample company of established British writers (Ian McEwan and Martin Amis are representative) have little or nothing to say about transcendence. When religion is broached in their works, it is regularly in terms of a simplistic opposition between faith and reason. Genuine rationality can become the first casualty of this attitude.

The blind spot is equally evident across a large patch of academia. For a snapshot of the times, consider the example of Iain McGilchrist, psychiatrist, literary critic and intellectual historian of distinction. In 2009, he published his magnum opus, *The Master and his Emissary: The Divided Brain and the Making of the Western World*.[5] The book is partly a work of neuroscience exploring left- and right-brained perspectives on the world. Put very simply, McGilchrist's thesis is that our valuing of left-brained capacities—problem-solving, for instance—tends to come at the expense of appreciation for the right brain's more elusive but equally important grasp of the big picture. McGilchrist admitted in private that his book is heavily religious in inspiration. Yet if this were highlighted, he warned, many scholars would not bother to read it. In recounting this anecdote, I do not mean to imply that the direction of travel is uniform. Religious studies is now treated more seriously in English-speaking countries than two generations ago, when sociologists and others tended to see the investigation of faith communities as akin to examining dead civilisations. Philosophers with Christian allegiances such as Charles Taylor, Jean-Luc Marion and Alasdair MacIntyre are internationally renowned. So, too, are theologians including John Milbank, Sarah Coakley and Rowan Williams, to cite just three British names. But McGilchrist's comment is nevertheless telling. The blinkers have yet to come off in some quarters.

Though sometimes associated with the political Left (a survey several years ago revealed that Richard Dawkins's polemic *The God Delusion*[6] was especially popular reading material among Labour MPs), disdain for religion in general and Christianity in particular is by no means confined to one side of the spectrum. Right-leaning figures in England such as Toby Young, Matthew Parris, Dominic Lawson and Michael Portillo can be as dismissive of faith as some of their political foes. Young, for instance, has used his column in *The Spectator* to describe spiritual belief systems as 'nonsense on stilts'. Anyone who considers my frames of reference parochial should read *Absence of Mind*,[7] Robinson's penetrating critique of allied attitudes on her side of the Atlantic. The author was prompted by far more than journalistic needling. Behind her project stand more committed if no less one-sided critics of religion than Dawkins, especially the neuroscientist Sam Harris,[8] the philosopher Daniel Dennett,[9] and Christopher Hitchens,[10] journalist and man of letters. Loosely known as the New Atheists, they have mounted the most pugnacious intellectual assault on Christianity in many decades. These men are able sword-wielders, but less handy with scalpels.

Strictly speaking, questions about a cultural climate are at a remove from my main concern, which is to defend the coherence of Christian belief. Yet style and substance are notoriously hard to disentangle. Take another instance of the trend we are noting. Antony Flew, a leading academic exponent of atheism in the anglophone world during the second half of the twentieth century, announced a dramatic change of mind soon after the turn of the millennium. While emphatically refusing to embrace any religious creed, he had nevertheless come to accept on philosophical grounds that the universe was created. Despite his eminence, he acknowledged that he had never studied Aristotle's arguments for a First Cause in sufficient depth; his conclusion had been further buttressed by reflections on science. Among the factors accounting for this shift were the rationality implicit in all our experience of the world, consciousness, and the implications of conceptual thought. True to the maxim that an honest enquirer should follow the argument where it leads, Flew traced his evolution towards deism in *There Is a God: How the World's Most Notorious Atheist Changed His Mind*.[11]

The relative lack of novelty in his case has no bearing on its force. Thinkers of many different stripes have long judged that the building of a theological framework starts from our sense of ourselves as embodied beings with the capacity to understand meaning. Since it is hard to deny, consciousness provides a ready vehicle for discrediting materialism. The point is well captured in an exchange reported about the philosopher Paul Ziff, involving himself and an Australian materialist called Armstrong:

> *Armstrong*: There is only one type of thing in the world, like neutrons.
>
> *Ziff*: What about the number 17?
>
> *Armstrong*: I was never any good at mathematics. Let's have a drink.[12]

Ziff's point does not necessarily point towards theism, of course. But at the very least it should pose a challenge to the thought police seeking to censor all talk of the transcendent. Flew's *There Is a God* met with indifference and sharp hostility, as well as enthusiasm. Another philosopher, Edward Feser, begins *The Last Superstition*,[13] his rebuttal of New Atheist standard-bearers, with examples of the ad hominem attacks directed at Flew—some focusing on his age—as well as the many distortions of his message. The failure of evangelical unbelievers to engage with the meat of Flew's arguments is very striking. Much the same applies to debate on the work of Thomas Nagel, author of *Mind and Cosmos: Why the Materialist Neo-Darwinian Conception of Nature is Almost Certainly False*,[14] even though Nagel (a scholar of the first rank) has not resiled from his atheism. I write soon after publication of the geneticist Jerry Coyne's *Faith vs Fact: Why Science and Religion are Incompatible*.[15] Neither Flew, Feser nor Nagel appears in Coyne's index; there is a fleeting reference to David Bentley Hart, an Eastern Orthodox thinker Coyne wrongly describes as a liberal.

Hart's books include *Atheist Delusions*[16] and *The Experience of God*,[17] widely seen as two of the most formidable essays in intellectual history and philosophical theology by a living author. I have also searched in vain for sustained comment on the immensely important arguments of historical figures—principally St Thomas Aquinas—in New Atheist publications. Dawkins's treatment of the subject is as brief as it is flawed; what is true of an area such as Thomism applies no less strongly to the Bible.

Though Feser and Bentley Hart are no strangers to the withering put-down, both pay their opponents the compliment of examining the case against God in detail. So do other weighty figures, including Alister McGrath in *The Dawkins Delusion?*,[18] John Polkinghorne in works such as *Science and Christian Belief*[19] and *Science and Religion in Quest of Truth*,[20] Janet Martin Soskice in *The Kindness of God*,[21] Keith Ward in *The God Conclusion*[22] and, employing a different register, Francis Spufford in *Unapologetic*.[23] All this points towards a bracing but in my view accurate conclusion. With its insistence on uniformity of thought, hardline secularism now resembles a species of dogmatic religion in some respects. Daniel Dennett has gone so far as to suggest that atheists should be called 'brights', to distinguish them from religious believers.[24] If you are genuinely open-minded, you do not need to insult your opponent's intelligence or confine yourself in a mental silo. One would hardly suppose from all this that the great majority of Western scientists and philosophers in recent centuries have been theists, or that claims like 'matter is all that exists', and 'empirical science is the only path to knowledge', have been repeatedly found wanting by a large number of Ziff's and Nagel's precursors.

If anti-religionists share one other major assumption bearing on this apology for a conversation, it is that the god in whom they disbelieve is a redundant thing serving no explanatory function for the scientifically informed observer. One of Dawkins's most astonishing claims is that a creator of the world would need to be complex, that this complexity would need to arise from natural selection, and that there is no evidence for the evolution of any being more exalted than humanity so far.[25] The god pictured here is thus a product of the universe, as well as its creator—perhaps a kind of demiurge. To describe the notion as confused is an acute understatement.

A Christian response to the New Atheism should make clear among much else that the Creator represented in orthodox teaching is not a thing, or any part of reality as we understand it. The Catholic theologian Herbert McCabe had a tart rejoinder to those who imagine that you can add God and the universe together and make two. 'Two what?' Divinity and creaturehood are too different to be opposites. They do not occupy any kind of common scale. For a figure such as Aquinas, faith does not rest on supernatural awareness of ethereal entities in the way atheists often suppose. As the scientist and philosopher Timothy McDermott puts it, 'even our virtue is not directly perceptible to us. It is part of our interpretation of the world we perceive with our senses.'[26] So Aquinas was not concerned with some enchanted world beyond science's powers of disenchantment. 'He was interested in pressing more and more deeply into a scientific account of the natural,' McDermott adds, for 'already in that world there were things which only his religion would be able to explain.'[27]

Please do not suppose that I underestimate the intellectual appeal of Darwinism, or that I imagine the questions raised by Dawkins and Coyne at their most constructive can be swept aside. There is grandeur in their vision; it presents genuine challenges to the believer. One is that processes of life evolve over very long periods, so that human beings only emerged shortly before midnight on the clock of history. Another is that evolution is an unintended process arising from random mutation. Even if you deny that these factors point ineluctably towards atheism, they do chip away at the idea, much repeated in Judeo-Christian history, that humans are a little lower than the angels. Dawkins, Coyne and others are certainly right to expose the ignorance and charlatanism of assorted fundamentalists, whose easily disposable certainties now form one of atheism's main assets. Granted all this, the question remains whether an intellectually robust case for Christianity can still be made without watering down the main tenets of the faith. I believe that it can.

* * *

To say more about culture or philosophy at this stage would be to anticipate. But several other areas deserve an immediate mention in this overview. One is that although rates of churchgoing have fallen steeply in Europe over recent decades, secularisation in the world as a whole has gone into reverse. Almost all other societies display high levels of spiritual belief and practice. Religion is not going to disappear; religious literacy is hardly an optional extra.

Side by side with this (and much more familiar) lies the deeply troubling rise of faith-tinged violence, especially among Islamist extremists, who stand out so starkly from the overwhelming majority of their fellow Muslims. The Church is regularly tarred with the same brush. In her book *Fields of Blood: Religion and the History of Violence*,[28] the historian Karen Armstrong has observed that large numbers of people—'American commentators and psychiatrists, London taxi drivers and Oxford academics'— cite undifferentiated 'religion' as the cause of all the major wars in history. The short-circuiting of debate by unacknowledged ideology is no less clear here than when militant atheists pillory believers with straw-man arguments and half-truths in the media. What cries out for greatest explanation is not war, which is plainly a result of our evolutionary past, but the rejection of armed conflict preached by Jesus. The sweeping away of eye-for-an-eye morality in the Sermon on the Mount was often overlooked after Christianity became the official faith of the Roman Empire. Christians could naturally be as violent and intolerant as today's jihadists on occasion, though the Church's just-war tradition evolved in stages over the following millennium and has been greatly refined during the past century. When secular humanists attack Christianity, they often fail to realise that it is the gospels which provide unseen elements in their own outlook. A critical distinction between good and bad religion is lost along the way.

Conceived as a tract—pithy but not, I hope, glib—this book consists of five interlaced essays. The next traces the shape of a Christian worldview. The others deal respectively and in more detail with the conceptual, spiritual and political themes sketched in Chapter 2. One of my aims is to shed light on what is and is not central to Christianity, and on why the questions at stake are pivotal to human flourishing. Others will naturally attach different levels of weight to this or that topic, even though I have largely avoided matters on which Christians can disagree in good conscience, such as church order or the place of the sacraments. So no claim to comprehensiveness is being made. Many more detailed expositions of philosophical theology and of doctrine are already available. Nor have I attempted a frame-by-frame response to the New Atheists: this ground is also well trodden. The goal is rather to turn the soil at some of the most prominent spots in a large field. When the cavils of religion's cultured despisers are cited, it is usually to lay bare what strike me as mistaken or over-hasty verdicts on the themes in question. I hope that my willingness to take issue with both liberal and conservative Christians at some points, as well as with sceptics, will be seen in part as a mark of good faith. And although writing especially for those who find the creeds unpalatable or plain baffling, I have no sense of missionary fervour. If the open-minded are encouraged to take Christian perspectives seriously, if a waverer finds encouragement, or if the already committed are helped with honing their beliefs, my hopes will be largely met.

Here, perhaps, lies the rationale for another defence of the faith. Granted, the Church is more than able to take care of itself—because its ranks are boosted by thousands of adult converts a day worldwide (not to mention baptised infants); because naturalism, scientism and other so-called weapons of mass deconstruction are not as tenable as many atheists suppose; and above all because self-critical Christianity is a pearl of great price. Granted, too, I lay no claim to originality as usually understood. The coming pages draw freely on the resources of tradition. There is much insight in the adage that the original is one who returns to the origins; the green pastures along the way afford some invigorating views.

RESETTING THE COMPASS

Any bid to commend the claims of Christianity in writing should include a critical caveat. This book defends a way of life, not a scientific theory such as evolution, or an abstract term like liberty. Whatever view you take of my theme, it cannot be divorced from the personal commitment that gives it its meaning. Like some of the ancient philosophical schools, religion is a path of understanding which can say little to those who have not set out on the journey. Disengaged study misses the point: it is like analysing a poem in terms of the chemistry of the ink on the page.

This thought leads to my main coordinates. You don't think your way into a new way of living, but live your way into a new way of thinking. Being a Christian should not entail assenting to six impossible propositions before breakfast, but doing things that change you. The practical witness of believers may be their most eloquent statement of faith. G. K. Chesterton got right to the point when he described his creed as 'less of a theory and more of a love affair'. Now consider the contrast between all this and much English-language philosophy, which tends to neglect the big picture.[1] I would rather follow the lights of earlier thinkers including Cicero—especially his belief that the only fulfilling model for life rests on altruistic endeavour—and later figures who Christianised some of the noblest strands in pagan thought by adding the key precepts on love of God and neighbour.

So the old warning to producers of agitprop—show, don't tell—applies on my patch as well. The heart has its reasons; there is a limit to what can be established through argument. The number of people who come to faith as a result of intellectual exchanges alone is fairly small. Yet recognising the limit of a project is not to suggest that it lacks value. We have seen that Christianity is facing a sustained intellectual attack, not least through serving as a lightning rod for more general forms of anti-faith invective. A sense that a high proportion of the fire-breathers now belong in the atheist camp is forcefully conveyed by Francis Spufford in *Unapologetic*. He starts the book by telling us that his daughter, just turned six, will soon discover 'that her parents are weird. We're weird because we go to church.' In other words, Spufford explains, she will be told with increasing vehemence over the years ahead that her parents believe in a load of bronze-age absurdities, or that they're dogmatic, or savagely judgemental, that they fetishise pain and suffering while believing in wishy-washy niceness, and are too dumb to understand the irrationality of their convictions. If you think this reaction is overblown, just look at the cascades of anti-Christian ranting dignified as 'Comment' on even quality-newspaper websites. Bigotry is harder to brush aside when it is symptomatic of a broader malaise. An American historian and agnostic who has lived in England and elsewhere in Europe for many years summed up her diagnosis like this. 'I've always seen Christianity as involving an encounter with the depths of experience,' she told me. 'Yet so many educated people on this continent seem to associate it with nothing beyond the shallows.'

I share Spufford's outlook. In a modest way I also straddle the domains of journalism and letters, in which few practise a faith. I am regularly cross-questioned about my beliefs at social gatherings by slightly bewildered people who consider me normal in other respects; and one of the first things I feel bound to point out is that I don't recognise my credo in the caricatures often peddled on the other side of the debate. No, the Church does not teach that God is a celestial headmaster, even if some preachers have done a good job of projecting their fantasies and guilt feelings into the sky and giving them a holy veneer. If God is no thing, then God is not an agent whose actions compete with those of other agents. And by the way, the New Testament is a pretty anti-religious collection of books in some respects. It asks us to set aside most conventional images of the divine: to think in terms of a Creator who took off his crown in coming to share our flesh. Penitent Christians do not (or should not) confess their sins in order to *obtain* forgiveness. They do so because they are *already* forgiven. That

15

is the insight underlying the doctrine of justification by grace shared by the mainstream Protestant, Catholic and Orthodox traditions alike.

Christianity is not meant to be flawed science, even though some believers play into the hands of their critics by implying that it is. If God is simply an expedient for plugging ever-shrinking gaps in our knowledge, then I am an atheist as well, and so are many abler advocates of faith. The religion-as-bad-science fallacy derives from scientism: an insistence on forcing all truth onto a scientific template. If you think that the only meaningful utterances are either mathematical or provable in a test tube, then you're rejecting ethics, aesthetics and much of culture, as well as spirituality.

But let me try to be as fair as possible to my dining companions. Their questions are nothing if not vital. They may be appalled at the role of religion in fomenting conflict (if a little anxious that singling out one body in discussing the world's current woes will draw charges of Islamophobia); or rightly outraged by faith-tinged misogyny and the hounding of gay people down the centuries—injustices that obviously persist; or alarmed by the rejection of scientific rationality evident in some parts of the Christian world; or concerned that religion is given a privileged place in the public square. And they may of course just think that confident talk of agencies and perspectives beyond the tangible is silly at best.

Given the size of this menu, I shall need to crave your patience in fashioning a set of counter-arguments through a look at different areas in turn. If we were to trace a common thread in the views of the more historically minded of hardline secularists, a group including Christopher Hitchens, it might run like this. When Western Christendom was at its zenith during the Middle Ages, people were overwhelmingly ignorant and superstitious. Science and other forms of learning wilted. Witches and heretics were burned at the stake. The achievements of Greece and Rome lay discarded. The better informed will salute the medieval Islamic scholars who promoted study of Plato and Aristotle, thereby helping to reverse the tide and usher in the Renaissance. The Reformation formed another positive development, in part because it unwittingly accelerated Christianity's eclipse. The rebirth of science was followed by political enlightenment. Western societies reached adulthood; the theocratic schemes of clerics were kept at bay by the separation of Church and State. In time, all sensible people will share the outlook of modern men and women who have 'come of age'.

This narrative has almost attained the status of a humanist catechism. But while not totally false, it stands in need of heavy qualification. Far from destroying classical texts, Christian monasteries preserved many of them, helping to save Western civilisation during the Dark Ages. Learn a little about the Oxford calculators of the fourteenth century, for example, and you can see impressive continuities between medieval and Renaissance science.[2] Before resisting Galileo—a battle more attributable to the clash of combative individuals than to scientific matters as such—the Catholic Church had repudiated biblical cosmology in favour of a Greek model based on the movement of the spheres. (Incidentally, orthodox

17

Christianity does not hold the Bible to be factually iner-
rant. Scripture itself nowhere claims such a status. And
the Protestant fundamentalism on which the New Atheists
rely for plausibility is a new kid on the block in historical
terms, owing much to culture wars in the United States.)
What's more, intellectual historians worth their salt will
tell you that the discoveries of Newton, Galileo, Kepler
and Copernicus marked not so much a liberation from
religious authority as a break with long-dominant aspects
of Aristotelianism—a move already triggered in the later
Middle Ages.

Secularists who upbraid the Church over horrors such
as the Crusades and the seventeenth-century wars of
religion are on solid ground. But they tend to overlook
the huge role of the State in stoking strife. Even in the
seventeenth century, violence increased in proportion to
the amount of sovereignty claimed by the State—and
for the scale of their violence, twentieth-century atheistic
regimes exceeded anything witnessed during the periods
of church ascendancy. In a powerful discussion of this
subject, David Bentley Hart has observed that:

> The Thirty Years War [1618–48], with its appalling toll of
> civilian casualties, was a scandal to the conscience of the
> nations of Europe; but midway through the twentieth century
> … even liberal democracies did not scruple to bomb open
> cities from the air, or to use incendiary or nuclear devices to
> incinerate tens of thousands of civilians.[3]

As Bentley Hart realises, the case for the defence
extends deeper than this. Pre-Christian religion regularly
mandated self-mutilation and human sacrifice. The
weak were despised. Christianity's stress on the radical

equality of all, and the founding of hospitals, schools and other philanthropic institutions, were genuinely revolutionary. Legislation enacted under Roman emperors such as Theodosius II and Constantine raised the status of women. Even slavery—an institution common to all pre-modern societies that reached a certain level of wealth—was described as blasphemous as early as the fourth century by Gregory, Bishop of Nyssa. Though the blasphemy persisted for a further 1,500 years, it was finally curtailed on the initiative of Western Christians.

I do not say all this to score points, still less to exonerate the Church. Human beings are naturally rapacious. We display a dangerous thirst for unreality, which is another way of saying that we are sinners. Often misconstrued as a spurious notion based on moralising dogma, sin is the basic empirical reality that Christian teaching responds to and makes sense of. This is why the correct definition of a Christian is not a good person, but someone who acknowledges their *failure* to be good. The most authentic strands in the Christian repertoire—peace, forgiveness, joy, meekness, purity of heart, solidarity—have infiltrated societies without necessarily changing them at root. This should not surprise us. The Church regards itself as both a divine society instituted by Christ, and as a human society with a sometimes terrible history. According to Jesus in Matthew 13, the sifting of the wheat and the tares will be carried out by God alone in the fullness of time.

I am even less keen to disparage the achievements of non-Christian pioneers and cultures. Democracy was invented in the ancient world; goods such as freedom of speech derive mainly from the Enlightenment. We owe much to many sorts of forebear. But I *am* concerned to question lazy or ill-informed readings of history, and I worry about the assumption that we can preserve what is best in Christianity while abandoning belief in God. Principles such as human rights and human dignity may not automatically survive once commitment to the infinite value of every life has faded away.

Meanwhile, let us at least concede that Christianity deserves a hearing, even though Christians themselves should display due humility, given the Church's patchy record. If you think this sounds wishful, or that I am gazing down the well of history and simply catching my own reflection, then let me caution that a pillar of orthodoxy such as Aquinas thought a balance needed to be struck between the twin vices of too much religion and too little. I have already implied that aggressive secularism displays the second of these vices, while fundamentalism—what Aquinas would have called superstition—belongs in the first. The Church is not incapable of error; its representatives can easily make statements going far beyond the basic natural perception of the mystery of existence. Such statements can lead to mistakes, conflict and other evils, including the idolisation of community identities. In certain respects, the history of religion maps onto the entire social history of humanity. One implication of this is that religious leaders function better as sources of influence at some distance from political leaders, not as wielders of direct power themselves. Correspondingly, while faith groups should be allowed to express their views on the issues of the day, they should not undermine the democratic process. Roman Catholicism is not the only branch of Christianity to have had difficulties with this idea, though its record has improved greatly since the Second Vatican Council, 1962–5.

I have argued that the performance of the Church is not in itself evidence for the truth or falsity of the creeds. So although the ground-clearing so far has been necessary, it is also at a tangent to my main theme. Let us return to the inquisitorial dinner parties. When the subject of intellectual history has been broached, I have regularly been drawn back to biology and cosmology. I accept Darwin's world-transforming idea, and emphasise that I have learnt much from the professional writings of Richard Dawkins. But our focus is not on Dawkins the distinguished zoologist, but on his status as a poor student of theology. Science tells us about the connections between phenomena. It explains *how* this or that process has taken place, but cannot say *why*. Christians, Jews, Muslims and other monotheists see God as the answer to a quasi-scientific conundrum only in the sense that they do not think that the world made itself. The shape of classical arguments on this point will absorb us in the next chapter.

For now, we can note a sharp cleavage between those who see no special significance in the fact that there is something rather than nothing, and others who view the very existence of the world as profoundly suggestive. In his book *A Universe from Nothing*,[4] the atheist physicist Lawrence Krauss only acknowledges in passing that his account of how the world emerged from 'nothing' assumes the prior existence of a quantum vacuum (lowest energy state). But where did *this* come from? You cannot have something unless something else gives. That is scientific truth as understood both by an ancient pioneer such as Aristotle, and by science today. For a believer, of course, the ultimate source of all is God. It is not unreasonable for the atheist to counter that we cannot know about transcendent reality, and no set of human scales is equal to the task of weighing questions about the final ground (if any) of creation. In reply, the three Abrahamic faiths underline the widespread impulse to push against the boundaries of what can be said. Believing that the universe arose from nothing and that this cannot be explained in naturalistic terms, these traditions all hold that the world is related to a reality that does not stand alongside it, but in some sense holds or includes it.

Yet how can believers move from reasoning that the world was created to talking with any confidence about what critics often term their imaginary friend in the sky? We might start to answer this by noting a set of insights voiced by the philosopher Roger Scruton. Although he was a non-believer for decades, the final chapter of his memoir, *Gentle Regrets*,[5] is entitled 'Regaining my Religion'. It includes a cluster of suggestive insights. First, that there are certain truths about the human condition that are hard to formulate and hard to live up to, and which we therefore have a motive to deny. It may require moral discipline if we are to accept these truths and live by them. For instance, there is the truth that we are free, accountable and objects of judgement in our own eyes and in the eyes of others. Or that we are motivated not only by desire and appetite, but by a vision of the good.

Or that we are not just objects in the world of objects, but also subjects, who relate to each other reciprocally. Scruton adds that this way of looking at the world 'deploys concepts that are given to us through religion, and to be obtained only with the greatest difficulty without it'.[6] He has paraphrased the point elsewhere, pointing out that while many people are uninterested in technical arguments about the existence of God, they do ask questions about how to live. And in pursuing an answer, 'they often stumble upon moments, places, relationships and experiences that have a numinous character—as though removed from this world and in some way casting judgment upon it.'[7] Scruton is here echoing an idea found both in some contemporary philosophy and in much older thought: that aspects of reality—the face of another human being or an accomplished work of art, say—point to inexhaustible layers of meaning. Reflection on experience in the round sharpens awareness of a bottomless mystery, the most appropriate responses to which are awe, gratitude and a heightened sense of ethical imperatives.

Can philosophy shed any further light on the discussion before we are required to make a leap of faith? I think so. While Hegel is not always thought of as a theological thinker, some elements in his work offer tantalising resources to the Christian. Among them is the idea that the process of thinking entails a form of negotiation, and thus a degree of self-displacement, so that self-examined mental life requires a move away from solipsism and self-preoccupation. And (to simplify a more complex story), if thinking and loving are con-

23

nected, this might also give us purchase on the meaning of life.[8]

Gillian Rose (1947–95), the Jewish-born Hegelian philosopher and sometime Marxist, was baptised in the Church of England on her deathbed. Rowan Williams has built on Rose's ideas, arguing that 'mind', or powerful intelligence, is never creative by itself. 'Think of the Daleks', he once suggested to an audience embarking on the Alpha Course for religious enquirers. The *Doctor Who* reference was astute. What the then archbishop meant was that only a loving force could create something completely different and rejoice in that difference. 'Our existence as intelligent creatures—loving, risking, questioning—somehow fits with the idea that God is a God of loving intelligence, who loves what's different.'[9] There is no irresistible argument for the truth of this, so we are always left with the need for a step into the unknown of some kind (some call it a leap of the imagination). And for the Christian, the process is harnessed by listening to the words of Jesus and taking in what he does. Bit by bit, people piece the gospel elements together to arrive at the conviction that Christ is the revelation in a human life of what God is like. Conversion experiences vary: St Paul's was famously sudden. A more common Christian path includes taking biblical and church teaching about God and his gifts on trust, but then finding this move retrospectively vindicated by experience. It could hardly be otherwise, given the shape of my argument at the start of this chapter.

It is time to put a little flesh on historical claims about Jesus. Many liberal believers, let alone agnostics and atheists, have doubts about the reliability of the New Testament. An example comes in Alan Isler's novel *Clerical Errors*,[10] where a priest educated in the 1950s and 1960s loses his faith and speaks for many in asking, 'How can any rational creature not see in the story of Christ the pattern of countless pagan myths, the universal romance of the sacrificial god, his apotheosis and his rebirth?' This question has a period feel, a point overlooked in two recent fictional bestsellers, Colm Tóibín's *The Testament of Mary*[11] and Philip Pullman's fundamentally misconceived *The Good Man Jesus and the Scoundrel Christ*.[12] It isn't over-simplifying a complex picture to say that many scholars are more confident about the gospels' reliability than several generations ago. One robust summary of Jesus's message might run like this. In common with other rabbis, he expounded Scripture, enjoined his hearers to observe the central elements of Jewish law, and emphasised God's love for the outcast. More remarkable was his absolute renunciation of violence and insistence on self-giving love as the supreme virtue. He proclaimed the arrival of the Kingdom of God, with all that it entailed in terms of espousal of the poor and weak, the casting out of evil spirits, and the release of those resources of generosity and compassion which are so easily deflected by social convention and spiritual legalism. This mission led to Jesus's death, which he accepted, sensing that his crucifixion and subsequent vindication by God would have redemptive power for the community of believers he inaugurated.

He believed this because he made one especially audacious claim from the start of his ministry: that the question of how people relate to him and to what he says will govern how they relate to the God he addressed as Father. On this understanding, Jesus was acting like the Creator who chose Israel at the dawn of the biblical narrative. God had chosen a group of slaves to be a people; and Jesus, in selecting his fishermen, tax collectors and prostitutes, was repeating and re-embodying this choice. He was claiming a level of creative freedom for himself usually associated with God alone.

Christian experience was distilled from the experience of prayer and communal life over generations. The teaching that emerged in the New Testament and early Church holds that through Jesus's death and resurrection, a new phase in history has been inaugurated. Human beings discover their destiny in an orientation towards the source of their being; but this is not the orientation of a slave to a master, but the intimate relationship of a son or daughter to a parent. In that relationship, the Christian can become free to imitate the self-giving of God the Trinity—a pattern of loving relationship— who made us and saved us. The Church is the community on earth representing this 'new creation'. Its chief task is to proclaim and witness to God's will for universal reconciliation.

Why was Jesus crucified and why does it matter? One of the first things worth noting is that his execution was not accidental. He indicates several times in the gospels that his forthcoming demise cannot be avoided. This was not just because he scandalised the Jewish authorities by presenting his teaching as the fulfilment of the law of Moses, but also because of a more general human trait—

our tendency to despise and reject full humanity when we encounter it.

Jesus plainly did not want to die. His anguish in the Garden of Gethsemane is clearly recorded. Yet over and again, he is portrayed as wanting to do the will of his Father above all. This is not to suggest that the Father sought Jesus's death either. Commentators have drawn an analogy with human parenthood: mothers and fathers are aware that their children may suffer all manner of adversity given the slings and arrows of fortune, but it is not their wish that this should happen. What loving parents hope for is that their offspring will flower as people. The 'Father's will', of which Jesus was so conscious, consisted in being completely human: this was the path that led to the cross. In the words of Herbert McCabe, 'the fact that to be human means to be crucified is not something that the Father has directly planned but that we have arranged. We have made a world in which there is no way of being human that does not involve suffering.'[13] Jesus can be seen in this light as the most perfectly human person ever to have existed: for him, to live was to love.

Widely held to be no more than a distant event of no abiding significance, the crucifixion remains hard to interpret, even for many Christians. An evolutionary perspective can help. It is almost universally recognised that when humans advanced to form social structures, their increased power came with greater danger and greater opportunity, including the capacity for both murder and love—a further mark of the cleft in our natures explored in many a religious text, biblical and non-biblical. With these ideas in mind, we can revisit my comment at the start of this book that the New Testament is an anti-religious document in important respects. This emerges forcefully in the work of René Girard,[14] the French anthropologist who long saw religions in negative terms as sublimated forms of wrath. He meant that many ritual systems entail the scapegoating of a victim as a way of channelling a given society's tendency towards violence, and engineering 'peace' (more a cessation of hostilities purchased at great price) around the corpse of the victim, whether animal or human. Having assumed that Judaism and Christianity reproduced this corrupt pattern, Girard came to see that the opposite is true. Both Jewish rituals and the Christian Eucharist employ sacralised violence as structuring motifs, but there is a deep difference compared with other religious systems. Through the Hebrew Bible and into the New Testament, God is gradually dissociated from religious violence until the victim is wholly innocent in the case of Jesus. What is more, the figure on the cross claims to speak for God; Christians in turn are challenged to identify this scene of execution as the place where God stands. The 'price' paid through the crucifixion is not connected with placating the supposed anger of God. It has to do instead with the manner in which the bearer of God's nature takes on the result of human hatred. God is revealed not as the figure who expels us, but as the one whom we expel, and who allowed himself to be expelled so as to make of his rejection an example of what he is really like.

* * *

Little has been said so far about the corporate implications of Christian belief. The gospels do not set out a
particular programme, but it goes without saying that a
thirst for justice in all its dimensions—including environ-
mental stewardship—should be priorities for anyone
seeking to follow Jesus. I have already pointed out that
Christians were instrumental in ending the slave trade;
one might also instance the place of Catholic social
teaching in helping develop the trade union movement
and the European welfare state. Protestants, especially,
did much to forge the United Nations Declaration on
Human Rights. Faith-based conviction has mobilised
millions of people to oppose authoritarian regimes, usher
in democratic transitions, foster human rights, and relieve
suffering. In recent decades, religious movements have
helped end colonial rule and promote democracy in
Latin America, Eastern Europe, sub-Saharan Africa and
Asia. The UN's Millennium Development Goals owe
much to the biblical notion of jubilee. There is also a
robust theological case for gay equality, among other pro-
gressive reforms. Unaware of the distinction between
homosexual practice and homosexual identity, the
Hebrew Bible or Old Testament does not reckon with
stable, monogamous homosexual partnerships. Church
teaching could therefore be revised in accordance with
Scripture's underlying message about the link between
sex and commitment rather than in defiance of it. This
process is clearly under way in some quarters, though
too many Christians remain unwilling to distance themselves from a pernicious prejudice.

We shall return to political and social questions in the
final chapter, but you will already have guessed that I do

not think that Christians should back minimal forms of government, whatever the views of certain influential Republicans in the United States. Just think (to cite another contemporary example at random) of all the evidence linking the removal of lead from petrol with the steep falls in violent crime since the 1980s. Another implication of my case is that faith communities are justified in giving public voice to their beliefs through foundations such as church schools. I view efforts to restrict these establishments—which in Britain do much to serve the wider population, not just a core constituency—as marks of secular authoritarianism. At the same time (and here I am conscious of writing in very general terms), the thoughtful believer should always be aware of the limits of public policy. Private behaviour matters deeply—more so than most politicians are allowed to say.

I conclude this sketch with a tribute not to a theologian but to an unconventional novelist—Nicholas Mosley—whose deceptively simple book, *Experience and Religion*,[15] helped focus my thoughts some years ago. Like many a balanced observer, he sees that there is space for grown-up Christianity between scepticism and fundamentalism. His outlook is expressed with a humility reflected in a use of parentheses: 'the world has meaning, is tragic: man can alter it (redeem). This is the point (it is done for him) in religion.'[16] Mosley shares a sense that Christianity offers the solidest foundation for values such as love, hope, truth and freedom, though this need not in any way preclude an open-handed attitude towards secularists and other faith groups. Some will still see an intellectual land grab in this claim. In my eyes, it rests on the search for a fundamental and inclusive context of meaning. To the goods just listed, I would add the impulse to solidarity, and with it a grasp of symbols. When a fascist paints a swastika on a synagogue, the wrong done goes beyond the cost of cleaning up and repainting. Understanding the symbolic and communicative dimensions of existence takes us beyond the world of cause and effect. What is the alternative to this vision? For Mosley, it is that 'everything might be ridiculous'.

I hope that these arguments will not be misinterpreted. The opposite of faith is not doubt, but certainty. Christians cannot know for sure that their creed is true in every particular; all serious religious practice ought to involve healthy doses of self-criticism; your conscience is in any case the final arbiter in this debate. But Mosley's warning is a variation on the theme spelt out with greatest force in the modern era by Nietzsche. The father of contemporary atheism was at least right about the height of the stakes. Yet he was at root profoundly mistaken. Other aspects of unbelief relate to philosophical and scientific conundrums which deserve more of an airing than they tend to receive outside academia. To grasp our intellectual inheritance more clearly—and perhaps reframe it—we must take an indirect path by reconsidering some of the main currents of Western thought from their beginnings.

3

GOD IS NO THING, BUT NOT NOTHING

Several of my main refrains will now be familiar. So much pooh-poohing of Christianity in our time rests on a series of parodies. Richard Dawkins et al. literally don't know what they are talking about, because the god they reject is an idol resembling a blown-up creature. Science is an exceptionally important mark of human civilisation, but its remit is not all-encompassing. On the contrary, scientism is a sitting duck. For a proposition such as 'the only meaningful statements are those deriving from natural science' is not itself a proposition of natural science. In other words, whether the claim is true or false, it follows that there is at least one fact which isn't a physical fact. This was the basic lesson apparently learnt after the bubble of logical positivism burst before the Second World War.

Howlers aside, the broader ramifications are especially worthy of note. It is not just scientists such as Dawkins, but also many philosophers (Richard Rorty being a notable example) who fail to see that secular humanism is not a neutral standpoint. It is an alternative metaphysical vision revolving around what a more searching thinker, Charles Taylor, has called 'images of power, or untrammelled agency, of spiritual self-possession'.[1] We will return to this vision and its very mixed legacy more than once.

The imperialistic aspirations of scientism influence other disciplines besides philosophy. Though partly infected by relativism, the humanities have also witnessed an urge to redescribe everything in material and supposedly objective terms. This can be profoundly mistaken; it involves restricting us to a world of causes rather than reasons, sounds rather than music. The impulse to apply science beyond its province is especially tempting in the case of evolutionary theory, because its repertoire is so flexible, embracing elements including adaptation and competition. Yet as the unspeakable things done in the name of Social Darwinism illustrate, it can be very dangerous indeed to employ biological categories outside the biological realm.

The fallacy of a scientistic or positivist approach was well brought out in a public debate between Richard Dawkins and John Habgood, then Archbishop of York, as far back as 1992.[2] If you search the universe for certain kinds of connections, those are the only ones you will find, Habgood warned. Everything else slips through the net. God does not appear in the scientific account of nature, because the objectives and methods of science shut out anything—any hint of purpose or intention or feeling or value—which might point to a Creator. That is not a criticism of science. It is a description of what science is, and the key to what makes it so successful in studying those aspects of reality in which purpose, feeling, value and so on are not of central importance.

Religious language points to truths that elude scientific treatment, but this should not render it invalid by definition. Take a ready parallel. Our understanding of others, not as objects to be analysed but as persons to be encountered, is just as real as our knowledge of stars or genes—more so, in fact, because it is more direct and involves a greater spread of our capacities. Aristotle had already made this kind of insight clear well before the birth of Christianity in his *Nichomachean Ethics*. Educated people do not expect the word 'certain' to mean the same thing in every context, he argues, adding that it is the mark of a juvenile to think that certainty is fully contained in the notion of mathematical certainty. Mathematics poses no difficulty for a 'juvenile' in this sense. But ethics is difficult, even for a mature person, because certainty isn't so easy to come by. You have to grow into it.

Philosophical roots and shoots

Since these points touch as much on philosophy as on religious belief and science, it seems right to step back by looking further at the ways in which some secular ideas are themselves the offspring of questionable developments within Christianity and the pre-Christian era. I am clear that there are less helpful forms of Christian (let alone atheist) thinking. As we have seen, Christians can play into their critics' hands by promoting just the model of God that atheists are right to shun. But it seems equally plain to me that the answer to bad theology is better theology, not no theology at all.

The tendency of believers to go adrift on occasion has something to do with a chain of ideas heavily influenced by Platonism, rather than biblical teaching. For instance, the atheist conviction that human beings are one thing—matter—is taken to be a result of rejecting what is seen as Christian orthodoxy—that we are two separate things, namely matter and spirit. Both of these models, the physicalist and the dualist, are mistaken.

One sketch of the terrain in question runs as follows. From Aristotle, we learn that very early Greek science, pioneered by figurers such as Democritus, tended to picture the world as simply atoms in perpetual motion; and that Socrates and Plato, Aristotle's precursors, reacted against this, in part by focusing on the human dispositions towards goodness and truth-telling. Plato held that his 'Forms' or 'Ideas' (as he termed categories including the true and the good) corresponded to an unchanging spiritual domain only faintly perceptible in the material world. Our capacity to perceive the eternal spiritual realm is, for Plato, a mark of our possessing immortal souls which are temporarily yoked to our bodies during our time on earth.

Aristotle rejected the dualism of Plato, insisting that human beings should be understood as psychosomatic unities. He also believed knowledge to be based on empirical observation rather than spiritual illumination. As it happens, Aristotle's model of the human person is closer to that of the Old Testament—and thus to Jesus's own setting—in important respects.[3] But Plato's vision nevertheless proved more attractive to some early Christian thinkers, partly because the Roman Empire was heavily marked by a Platonic stamp. For over a millennium after his death in 430, St Augustine ranked as the most influential thinker in the Latin Church; among much else, he helped recast Platonism in Christian terms. The works of Aristotle were duly reabsorbed in the West thanks to a rich process of intellectual cross-fertilisation involving Muslims, Jews and Christians in medieval Spain and elsewhere.

This is the background against which the work of St Thomas Aquinas (1225–74) took shape. Much of his achievement derives from seeing in Aristotle's stress on mundane, empirical processes a far stronger pointer to God than could be gained from Plato's appeal to the world of the spirit. In Aquinas's eyes, nature does not play second fiddle to supernature: God is not supernatural in the usual way the word is understood, but the source and end of the natural. Aquinas thus holds that human reason has its own God-given autonomy. Rejecting the separation of faith and reason, he sees the two as complementary means of shedding light on the truth of our being.

The current battle over religion and science is in some ways another variation on the old Platonic–Aristotelian clash. We have already pointed to a common assumption among Dawkins and his followers—that theologians are trying to add something on to what is already perfectly explicable by science. As also noted, however, a figure like

Aquinas is not going outside nature in this simplistic sense. He is asking, where does nature get it from? How is it all possible? Timothy McDermott makes the point with characteristic incisiveness: if we *were* to call God supernatural it would not be because he is 'extra-natural', but 'because he is the author of nature itself, and so both inside and outside it'.[4] Were Aquinas alive now, McDermott judges, 'he would surely have recognised the same struggle of secular and sacred, reason and revelation, material atomism and Platonic reality, in which he was [also] embroiled'.[5] From a Christian point of view, then, Aquinas's Aristotelianism offers a key for resolving common muddles and taking us forward.

To grasp the abiding relevance of Aristotelian categories, think of an example like a football match. The players are made up of molecules and larger physical parts (their matter), but they bring to bear a skill to galvanise their bodies and make real their potential (form, in Aristotle's sense). Combining matter and form, every creature displays an allied facility by dint of surviving in the world; and what is true of animals applies analogously to devices and machines. The function or 'form' of a button consists in its attachment to a piece of clothing. This function cannot exist apart from the material the button is made of, and the two sides of the garment it holds together. Yet the work the button performs is not merely a physical part of it.

So according to Aristotle (whose perspective connects with important strands of Scripture), the mind is not a separate entity mysteriously harnessed to the body, but the particular manner in which a given animal interfaces with the general environment. Aristotle's principle of form in matter renders Plato's immaterial 'Forms' or 'Ideas' redundant. The human mind is a form shaping matter, rather than a gateway to the supernatural. This entails epistemic realism—the common-sense view that the world genuinely exists and our senses apprehend true knowledge of it. Our instinct in contemporary Western culture is to begin with the mind, then ask how our mental acts relate to our surroundings. By contrast, Aquinas, following Aristotle, starts with the external objects that evoke intellectual activity on our part, thereby fulfilling our capacities.

The place of humanity is especially worthy of note, given that we bring understanding to our position in the world. A lump of coal is in contact with its environment, but not conscious of it. A rose can react to external conditions, but not to external objects. Non-human animals are aware of external objects, but not of their place in the world as a whole. We, though, are sensitive not just to the way in which this or that entity affects us here and now, but also to an entity's place in the wider scheme of things and its capacity to generate a response in language.

That humans possess some faculties which develop as a result of external stimulation—faculties needing to grow within us before they can be fully activated from without—is especially salient. Being a mix of animal desires (what we want naturally) and rational desires (marks of our will), we bring our emotional and voluntary dispositions into play under the direction of practical reason in pursuit of fulfilment. The process operates in innumerable ways. For example, as thinkers in the twilight zone between faith and unbelief such as Iris Murdoch and Simone Weil remind us, good art may

require patience, attention and a degree of self-efface-
ment before we are properly placed to absorb it. We saw
in the previous chapter that this principle can also apply
to our engagement with those around us. Murdoch, Weil
and other twentieth-century philosophers, including
Edith Stein and Emmanuel Levinas, point to how established religious categories might be refreshed for uncom-
mitted or sceptical palates.

The implications of all this bear restating for two reasons in particular. First, because the idea of following
the grain of reality is still a stumbling block in a climate
too easily seduced by do-it-yourself ethics. But second,
because the idea of natural law has regularly been
misused by authoritarian Christians as a tool of social
repression. Reactionaries—think of the Grand Inquisitor
in Dostoevsky's *The Brothers Karamazov*, but also of real-life,
if less totemic, figures closer to home—can forget an obvious lesson of the gospels: that God has given us striking
degrees of freedom. Aquinas is careful to note the difference between the laws of nature (including instinct) and
natural law—more accurately termed natural lawmaking.
On the basis that secondary legal principles can be developed through the use of reason, Christians are called to
be laws unto themselves in a genuine sense.[6] This is plainly
a very long way indeed from the assumption that disciple-
ship involves submitting to a rule book.

How is it all possible?

Since Aquinas's overarching framework is biblical and
theological, his Christian allegiance leads him to go

beyond Aristotle in important respects. Loving our neighbour as ourselves takes us from the domain of prudence towards that of *agape* or self-sacrificial love. Self-surrender and self-realisation coincide in this context; service can give birth to perfect freedom, to cite the Book of Common Prayer's 'Collect for Peace', which itself echoes Augustine. (Our tendency to turn our backs on the good and embrace the bad in no way blunts the truth of these insights.) One theological difference between Aristotle and Aquinas needs particular emphasis. Aquinas holds that form cannot cause existence as such, because existence is on loan from a source. This notion is discussed in the so-called Five Ways,[7] his arguments for God's existence. One relevant factor is that the question of existence ought to have two parts. Suppose we ask about the being of a tree. There is plainly a scientific explanation for a tree's coming into and passing out of existence. But Aquinas wants to probe deeper by asking whether it can be that *everything* is contingent like the tree, or whether there must be a cause of all, whose being need not be accounted for. His answer is that some necessary being does exist, because the existence of a contingent universe would be inexplicable.

Among the doubters are those who hold Thomas guilty of an elementary logical fallacy known as the quantifier shift. To declare that 'every chain of causes must stop somewhere, therefore there is somewhere where every chain of causes must stop' is as erroneous as announcing that 'every person has a woman who is their mother, therefore there is a woman who is the mother of every person.' Thus the critics, Dawkins included,[8] suppose

41

Aquinas to be saying that everything has a cause. But in that case (so the argument runs), God must have one too, rendering the argument circular. Aquinas's view is more penetrating. He argues that *what comes into being*—namely what is contingent—must have a cause. He sees all causes observable in the universe as 'second causes', not in the sense that they come after a first cause and before a third, but in that they are derivative—that is, not self-caused. God, though, according to the monotheistic traditions, does not have a cause, because the divine existence is held to be necessary.

To appreciate the rationale for this belief, we must note Aquinas's contrast between an 'accidentally' ordered or *backwards* series of causes and effects, and an 'essentially' ordered or *downwards* series. An instance of the former would be a father begetting a son, who begets a son of his own, and so on. Each generation is independent, so to speak: if a father dies, his son can clearly continue to live and have offspring of his own. Now think of an 'essentially' ordered chain—a hand employing a stick to push a stone, for example. The stone moves because a stick is pushing it, the stick moves because it is being propelled by a hand. A fuller catalogue might add that the hand's potentiality is actualised by the mover's arm, that of the arm by the muscles of the person concerned, that of the muscles by his or her nerves, and so on in a sequence involving the nervous system as a whole, molecular and atomic structure, and the four fundamental forces in the universe. For Aquinas, the vital points are that all these elements come into play simultaneously; and that this kind of series must have a first member holding it in being *here and now*, unlike an accidentally ordered series, which might in principle (he grants) extend backwards in time forever.[9] Given Thomas's Aristotelian context, some of his scientific examples are of course outdated or wrong. I do not doubt that Darwinism swept away the top-down medieval cosmology taken for granted by Aquinas. But this has freed us to see another aspect of his scheme: a bottom-up conception of existence in which God is immediately present to every individual part of nature, moment by moment. In particular, the argument from 'motion' (what we would term change), the first of Aquinas's Five Ways, is judged sound by many contemporary philosophers. We have already noted Thomas's conclusion—that everything in the universe is held in being by a First Cause standing outside it. In technical language, everything material is a mixture of both 'essence' and 'existence'—*what* it is and *that* it is—but the entity at the source of all causation is not such a compound. This is a being—better conceived as Being itself—whose essence is to exist.

Another Aristotelian distinction just alluded to in passing—between actuality and potentiality—underlies consideration of form and matter. It puts further flesh on Aquinas's argument. One common example draws on an everyday object like a rubber ball. Its spherical shape and bounciness are aspects of its being. Yet the ball is potentially other things as well—sticky if you melt it, say. Aristotle maintains that the category of potentiality lies between existence and non-existence. Stickiness does not *cause* the ball to become soft: change comes about through the combination of a potentiality in the ball and an external force—in this case heat. Note a major implication of this point. We tend to see actuality and potentiality in tandem, but their relationship is not symmetrical. Aquinas aligns himself with Aristotle in holding that absolutely speaking, actuality is prior to potentiality: in other words, potentiality cannot exist on its own, but only when yoked to actuality.[10]

Some readers, Christians among them, may wonder why I have devoted so much space to these philosophical distinctions. Please bear with me. They take us to the heart of the matter, given the dubious bid by atheists to demonstrate that the world emerged spontaneously without the need of a creator, and thus that the existence of something rather than nothing poses no particular conundrum for the non-theist. When Lawrence Krauss uses the term 'nothing' in his discussion, it is productive in each case. If Aquinas is right, however, *potentiality is always the property of something actual*, rather than the other way round. And here we have perhaps the fundamental reason why there cannot be a naturalistic explanation of existence.[11]

The point has tended to be imperfectly grasped across the atheist camp. In his book *On Being: A Scientist's Exploration of the Great Questions of Existence*, the physical chemist Peter Atkins, one of Dawkins's allies, proves no more convincing than Krauss in accounting for existence. What Atkins calls a problem of the profoundest difficulty, namely the unfolding of absolutely nothing into something, is avoided by a claim that because the electrical charges and the angular momentums and the energies in the cosmos all add up to zero, absolutely nothing has only unfolded into nothing. Since nothing 'positive' has to be 'manufactured', there need be no 'positive, specific, munificent creation',[12] Atkins thinks. This is as if we argued that quarrying a huge pile of material didn't amount to anything, because the pile's height was exactly cancelled out by the quarry's depth. Wiser heads have been firm on this point, arguing that it is impossible, in the terms naturalism allows, to say how anything can exist at all. It is a philosopher, Denys Turner, who gives one of the sharpest definitions of absolute nothingness I have come across: '"Nothing" has no process, no antecedent conditions, no random fluctuations in a vacuum, no explanatory law of emergence, and, there being nothing for "something" to be "out of", there can be no physics, not yet, for there is nothing yet for physics to get an explanatory grip on.'[13]

Victor Stenger, another distinguished scientist and author of *God: The Failed Hypothesis*, shares Atkins's confusion in arguing that 'nothing' is an unstable concept— i.e. that 'something' can come out of it, and that 'nothingness' is perfectly symmetrical, because elements such as time, position and velocity are absent from the void.[14] This also involves treating 'nothing' as something. Atkins and his allies seem obliged to assume elements such as a structured space-time, a quantum field, and the laws of nature.

The logic of the atheist position is that the universe has always existed. But that idea is hardly unproblematic, because as Antony Flew's collaborator Roy Abraham Varghese has pointed out, no material thing observable in the universe has 'any inner logic of unending existence'.[15] The theist's view may be judged more reasonable: the universe does have an ultimate ground, namely the Creator, but while God's existence is inexplicable to us, it *is* explicable to God. Reason infers the existence of causes from the existence of effects, without always being able to infer the nature of the causes from the nature of the effects. What applies in mundane spheres is all the more applicable in a unique area of discourse such as creation.

You will recall my paraphrasing one of Aquinas's questions: how is it all possible? We now have the means of framing an orthodox Christian reply. Consider an action like heating a pan of milk on a stove. The process has prompted confusion among believers and non-believers alike in three ways. The first mistake is to think that the gas heats the milk and God is not involved at all; the second, that God heats the milk and the gas plays no part; the third, that God makes the gas act on the milk as a puppeteer moves a puppet, meaning that the gas does not exercise a power of its own. According to classical teaching in the Abrahamic faiths, the correct interpretation is more nuanced. As a canvas supports a painting or a singer holds a tune, so God makes the whole situation to exist: the gas, its power and its action on the milk. God and the gas work at different levels, not in competition.

This example in turn sheds light on a traditionalist understanding of creation—misconstrued by advocates of Intelligent Design as well as by some of their atheist critics. As far back as ancient Greece, naturalistic thinkers had judged the universe to be eternal on the basis

that something cannot come out of absolute nothingness. A good number of Aquinas's contemporaries thus
judged the Greek view to be incompatible with Christian
belief in creation. Aquinas again digs deeper in distinguishing between cause seen as natural change, and
cause in the sense of an ultimate bringing into being of
something from no antecedent state whatsoever. To be
the complete cause of the existence of something is not
the same as producing a change in it. In Thomist eyes,
God did not create the universe out of 'something'. That
is why creation from nothing (*ex nihilo*) involves a relationship of radical dependency, for our existence right
now would be impossible without the sustaining power
of God, even though nature possesses its own integrity.
Michael W. Tkacz's gloss on this is helpful:

> God causes natural beings to be in such a way that they work
> the way they do. Hippopotamuses give live birth because that
> is the sort of thing they are. Why are there such things as
> hippopotamuses? Well, nature produced them in some way.
> What way did nature produce them and why does nature
> produce things in this way? It is because God made the whole
> of nature to operate in this way and produce by her own
> agency what she produces. Thus, God remains completely
> responsible for the being and operation of everything, even
> though natural beings possess real agency according to the
> way they were created.[16]

These tools equip us to face a vital question posed in
Stephen Jay Gould's book *Wonderful Life: The Burgess Shale
and the Nature of History*.[17] (The Burgess Shale is a fossil
area in Canada showing now extinct branches of life.)
Part of Gould's point is that if the remote past—and

47

thus the lottery of life—could be re-run, then the appear-
ance of humankind would have been extremely unlikely.
Next week's weather is inherently unpredictable; what is
true of the contemporary climate applies all the more to
evolution over hundreds of millions of years. Christians
hold that the emergence of humanity was part of God's
plan, but this is not to imply that God engineered the
process by devising some temporal mechanism to ensure
it. Nor does it make sense to think that God inserts into
time from eternity some event independent of all temporal mechanisms.

A different perspective from Jay Gould's comes in the
work of a scientist such as Simon Conway Morris.[18] His
account deals with far more philosophically significant
questions about the nature of created reality and the
relation of the creature to it. He points out that the cam-
era eye has evolved separately in very varied species (in
octopuses, for example, as well as in mammals). There is
something about the nature of things—see-ability or
visual lucidity—that evolution explores and latches on
to. Conway Morris also writes about intelligence, which
has likewise evolved independently several times. That
would relate to an intellectual lucidity to things, which
evolution explores. The rationality of the universe affords
human rationality, if you will.

Some features of evolution that really matter (such as
interacting with the world and understanding it) might
be inevitable, while other factors, such as how many fingers we have, are not. Perhaps the whole of our body
shape is undetermined, although there has been some
speculation that an upright bearing is more compatible

with intelligence than a downward one. It could also be argued that there is something theologically significant about distinguishing between more and less contingent aspects of evolution. For if we want to maintain that the rational, loving, remembering creature is in God's image, then it is important to say that the 'image' is in knowing, loving and remembering, rather than in having two hands or ten fingers, or skin of any particular colour. It is a helpful pointer to what really matters and what counts as idolatry. This model clearly precludes acceptance of Intelligent Design as currently advocated in parts of the Christian world. Belief that God needs to micro-manage events from time to time is to assume that he is normally absent, rather than, as Augustine says, closer to us than we are to ourselves.

Contemporary theistic arguments under the spotlight

What of related theistic arguments arising in the present? The Cambridge physicist and priest John Polkinghorne draws on several factors which have a cumulative force, even if they are not logically coercive. He makes particular play of what we have already identified as the world's deep intelligibility. It is not surprising that evolutionary adaptation has led us to develop true beliefs, enabling us to survive. Humans need to know where food is, what is poisonous, where predators may lie in wait, and so forth. But modern science enables us to see more clearly than ever that our powers of understanding greatly surpass the needs of day-to-day existence. Quantum physics is an obvious example, along with curved space-time, the geometrical properties of which differ from Euclidean models. One of the pioneers of quantum theory, Paul Dirac, linked his discoveries to a sustained quest for beautiful equations, describing the process as a 'very profitable religion' to have followed. Polkinghorne's more tightly expressed inference has struck many observers as fair: 'The rational transparency and beauty of the universe speaks of a world shot through with signs of mind, and it is an attractive and coherent possibility to believe that this is so because the divine Mind of the Creator lies behind its marvellous order.'[19]

This again takes us to the idea that the universe was pregnant with the possibility of developed life from the start. From chemistry, we know that it is carbon which plays a crucial part in the structure of the long-chain molecules that form the foundation of life. If the laws of nuclear physics had varied only slightly, the chain would have ruptured. There would be no carbon, and thus no possibility of carbon-based life. Belief that the universe is a divine creation offers an obvious explanation of why the world is marked by anthropic potentiality, for that fact can then be understood as an expression of the Creator's plan.

Another argument cited by scientifically trained believers focuses precisely on the world's evolutionary character. The universe entails a dovetailing between contingency and regularity, and between necessity and chance. Development emerges at the edge of chaos, where the orderly and the disorderly interact. As Polkinghorne explains, the point is corroborated by biological evolution. If there were no genetic mutations but only order,

there would be no fresh forms of life. If there were con-
stant genetic mutations, causing only disorder, no species
could have become established for natural selection to
work on. That is why some theologians welcomed *The
Origin of Species* from the start. Aubrey Moore famously
declared that 'Darwin appeared, and, under the guise of
a foe, did the work of a friend.' God had achieved something better than making a ready-made world, Moore
believed. Instead, the Creator allowed creatures to make
themselves. Moore's successors have built on his insights,
urging that the freedom entailed by this model is an
intrinsic good, even though genetic mutation can sometimes lead to malignancy and suffering, as well as to
great benefits. John Haught, author of *God and the New
Atheism*, is a case in point. 'As the ultimate ground of
novelty, freedom, and hope,' he writes,

> the Christian God offers the entire universe as well as our-
> selves the opportunity of ongoing liberation from the lifeless-
> ness of perfect design. Evolution, therefore, may be under-
> stood, at a theological level, as the story of the world's gradual
> emergence from initial chaos and monotony, and of its adven-
> turous search for the more intensely elaborate modes of being.
> The God of evolution humbly invites creatures to participate
> in the ongoing creation of the universe. This gracious invita-
> tion to share in the creation of the universe is consistent with
> the fundamental Christian belief that the ultimate ground of
> the universe and our own lives is the … self-emptying generos-
> ity of God.[20]

Keen to distance themselves from a deistic model,
where God creates the world but duly becomes a kind of
absentee landlord, some Christian theologians go on to

ask whether science allows us to picture divine involvement in more robust ways. Polkinghorne sees in Niels Bohr's 'Copenhagen' interpretation of quantum physics—which holds Heisenberg's uncertainty principle to be a mark of radical or 'ontological' indeterminism, not just a matter of ignorance—a way to accommodate God's action in the world.

> To do so does not imply that the future is some sort of random lottery, but simply that there are more causal factors active in bringing it about than those which science can describe in its reductionist terms of the exchange of energy between constituents. It would be natural to suppose that these additional causal factors include the exercise of human agency and divine providential interaction, both taking place within the open grain of creative nature. What this discussion certainly shows is that physics has not established the causal closure of the world on its terms alone.[21]

Perhaps not, but the risk is that you end up talking about divine interaction as if it were just one more force among forces, or one more counter on the table. What Polkinghorne does very well is draw attention to remarkable features of the universe—features that might bring the atheist up short. To repeat: I would rather connect the natural to God, ask why things are intelligible in the first place, and then root the answer in creation.

The argument we have traced prompts a provocative but unavoidable question: can we conceive of all the capacities I have enumerated, and associated with the world's created status, *without* belief in God? The subject is considered pivotal by Alvin Plantinga, perhaps the world's leading analytic philosopher of religion, who has advanced a new rationale for the existence of God known as the evolutionary argument against naturalism. The basis of his case involves a distinction between adaptive behaviour and true beliefs. Evolution can explain the former, he thinks, but not the latter. His conclusion is that while no conflict exists between Christianity and science, there *is* a conflict between philosophical naturalism and science, because adherents of naturalism (including atheists) have no firm basis for believing that many of their statements genuinely map reality. The Darwinian view thus fatally undermines itself. If it is true, then the methods that support it are probably unreliable, meaning that we should not believe it...

In a published conversation with Plantinga,[22] I raised an objection expressed by some of his Christian critics, as well as by non-believers. The query centres on his assumption that the generation of reliable belief-producing mechanisms should not itself be part of evolutionary adaptation. This sort of reservation has also been voiced by Jerry Coyne in *Faith vs Fact*. But whether or not one is fully convinced by Plantinga, he nevertheless succeeds in highlighting something disquieting about the naturalistic picture of our human predicament. Various scholars have noted that in a naturalistic worldview there is no systematic connection between our possession of equipment that has turned out to be efficacious in the battle for survival, and our putative ability to track the truth in relation to our intellectual intuitions. The underlying point, as the philosopher John Cottingham urges,

is that it seems impossible for any philosopher to characterise our human situation with respect to the truth—the ways in which we have fallen short, the ways in which we are able to correct our mistakes—without implicitly assuming that we are indeed equipped to undertake the search for truth. And it is not clear that this assumption can be underwritten via the resources of evolutionary naturalism.[23]

In rejecting Plantinga's arguments, Coyne stresses the many abilities that emerge as a by-product of evolution. Yes, he concedes, doing mathematics would not have enhanced the fitness of our pre-literate ancestors. But once the human brain had reached a certain level of complexity, it was already performing many tasks unconnected with evolution. Nor is this a mark of special pleading, Coyne adds. Crows can solve complex puzzles; lyrebirds can imitate chainsaws and car alarms.[24] These are weak analogies, however, because Plantinga is talking about advanced abilities which float free from the world of contingency. And in any case, Coyne has missed the deeper point, brought out even more sharply by Cottingham than by Plantinga: irrespective of whether our human epistemic capacities point to God, there is a further question about *the realities that our capacities track*. If there is something about the nature of reality that makes certain truths true, then naturalism looks less credible.

Confronting the question of how life got started, Dawkins writes in *The God Delusion* that its origin was 'the chemical event, or series of events, whereby the vital conditions for natural selection first came about … Once the vital ingredient—some kind of genetic molecule—is in place, true Darwinian natural selection can follow.'[25] And in answer to the inevitable follow-up, namely how *this* happened, he adds,

Scientists invoke the magic of large numbers ... The beauty of the anthropic principle is that it tells us, against all intuition, that a chemical model need only predict that life will arise on one planet in a billion billion to give us a good and entirely satisfying explanation for the presence of life here.[26]

Inflationary models in cosmology suggest that the universe is vast and possibly even infinite. Given time, then, there is a high probability that a world consisting of particles crashing around blindly will in the end generate the structures that lead to life and consciousness. Those who view the likelihood of conscious life as low or very low may need reminding of the limits of our knowledge. Another philosopher, Gideon Rosen, makes the point well. 'Suppose we could reproduce the physical conditions of pre-biotic earth in a thousand vats and let each evolve for a billion years. In how many of these vats would we expect life to emerge? We have no idea.'[27]

Again, though, there is a wide hole not properly confronted by Rosen, Dawkins and other atheists. Rosen starts with the 'indisputable fact' that conscious beings such as ourselves are capable of moral and scientific knowledge, but does not discuss the problem of what the moral knowledge is knowledge *of*. The whole discussion is weighted towards epistemology—the theory of knowledge—when the fundamental question revolves around ontology or being: what does the cosmos have to be like for there to be moral truths which we can detect in the first place?

To encapsulate an argument shadowing this entire chapter, it is easier to make sense of moral and other non-empirical truths if they are held—or acknowledged—to be rooted in a transcendental object. Certain observers are especially swayed by the example of 'normativity': the principle that moral values don't just inform us of facts, but require us to behave in particular ways. Compassion and cruelty form strong examples. The goodness of the former and wrongness of the latter are clear to all right-minded people, whether they like it or not. Various philosophers have noted an important change in the intellectual landscape over recent decades. Two or three generations ago, many practitioners were subjectivists who saw moral beliefs as no more than a matter of projection. The discrediting of subjectivism opens up a question about where the source of moral value really lies. Some atheists may judge that ethics are simply a function of our nature: just as people will flourish physically by eating a balanced diet, they will prosper in other respects by behaving well. Yet we have already noted more than once that there is a flaw in human nature, a point widely acknowledged on both sides of the faith divide. Other secular thinkers have argued that moral values are simply *there*, in a way comparable to the truths of mathematics. This is hard to refute philosophically, but the theist is entitled to argue that belief in God provides a much more secure home for our impulses than the idea that moral truths somehow float around in a Platonic limbo.

A host of Christians would want to press further by distinguishing between the cardinal and theological virtues: prudence, temperance, fortitude and justice on the one hand; faith, hope and love on the other. You can argue for goods such as reciprocity and fairness on the basis of pure reason. But what about grace and forgiveness? A whole dimension of normativity is lost in a naturalistic framework.

The eye of faith

What status should reasoning of the kind sketched so far in this chapter possess for a Christian? Believers have themselves sometimes been as hostile to 'rationalistic' arguments for God's existence as atheists, on the basis that faith is a divine gift, not the product of an intellectual equation. The Bible takes a more nuanced view overall. Although Paul in Romans 1:20 can speak of how nature witnesses to God's glory, he also describes the divine identity as invisible. So we can infer an ultimate source and cause of all, as in Aquinas's Five Ways, but this is quite intentionally a minimalist understanding taking us to the threshold of full-bodied belief, not beyond it. There is certainly no iron rule requiring a Christian to be a Thomist: I have simply laid more emphasis on Thomistic categories because they strike me as especially constructive, and fashioned to develop common ground with non-believers. But this is not for a moment to deny that the illiterate believer who cries out to heaven in anguish or gratitude or joy may be very close to the God who eludes all human categories—and a good deal closer than scholars over-absorbed by technical constructs.

Atheists may find the mixture of reason and self-investment, objective and subjective, implied by this picture especially unappealing. As I have reported, some consider any attempt to move outside the empirical domain illegitimate in principle, basing their arguments on limits to

human discourse laid down by major Enlightenment figures such as Hume and Kant, whose outlooks also shadow
so much contemporary debate. Yet there is a deep ambi-
guity about the very process of legislating boundaries.
Kant portrays us as standing on an island—representing
the empirical domain—surrounded by a foggy sea—
standing for the so-called noumenal world of things in
themselves.[28] In other words, in defining the limits of
human knowledge, the Kantian has a notion of a possible
world beyond those limits. *Kant is talking about the boundaries
of knowledge, rather than of reality*. We may not be able to
navigate the foggy sea with confidence, but nor are we
able to declare it non-existent—a point also well developed by Cottingham.[29]

Paul K. Moser, author of *The Evidence for God*,[30] an
important recent study of this complex subject, draws
inspiration from a framework especially associated with
Luther, Pascal and Kierkegaard in the modern era.
Instead of seeking to fashion religious statements on the
Procrustean bed of 'objective' reason, this approach lays
much emphasis on the unique way in which God is held
to reveal himself. Pascal, especially, thought that God
can be expected to appear openly to those who truly
search for him, but to remain hidden from those who do
not seek. Moser agrees. He rejects the demand of militant atheists for 'spectator evidence' of God's existence
as though this most mysterious of quests could be
resolved under laboratory conditions. His work is presented as an expression of 'kardiatheology'. It is targeted
mainly at one's motivational heart, including one's will,
rather than just at the mind or the emotions. Whatever

its challenges, this path is clearly in tune with the gospel summons to newness of life.

Moser nevertheless insists that faith needs to be 'cognitively commendable', not contradictory or arbitrary. He also draws support from Paul, and especially the 'grace-based' forms of knowledge evident in a passage such as Romans 5:5—'Hope does not disappoint us, because God's love has been poured into our hearts through the Holy Spirit that has been given to us.' Personal commitment really is unavoidable. Both Paul and his followers become evidence for God's reality. We are now a long way from the 'neutral' terrain characteristic both of theist–atheist debate and of some philosophy of religion courses, but the process has been necessary in order to give us the tools for attempting an authentically Christian description of God. No effort to capture the ineffable in words can fully succeed, of course. But the answer given by Rowan Williams to the broadcaster Melvyn Bragg, combining both intellectual and spiritual threads, is among the most succinct one could hope for:

> God is first and foremost that depth around all things and beyond all things into which, when I pray, I try to sink. But God is also the activity that comes to me out of that depth, tells me I'm loved, that opens up a future for me, that offers transformations I can't imagine. Very much a mystery but also very much a presence. Very much a person.[31]

In other words, God is not to be thought of primarily as an unmoved mover or first cause (despite being so), but rather as an intimate presence in the life of the believer responding to a gift and a richness from beyond his or her imagining.

4

A FAITH OBSERVED

Reflection on the stirrings of the heart in religious con-
texts has now emerged as a leitmotif of this book.
Granted, the process can lead to closed-mindedness or
outright bigotry in some cases. But contemporary psy-
chologists and others have produced much interesting
research into how human understanding can grow from
a delicate interplay between the intellectual and emotional spheres of life.[1] The focus on philosophical questions in Chapter 3 should not obscure the breadth and
accessibility of a Christian outlook. It not only encom-
passes major strands of Platonism, Aristotelianism and
some of their main mutations in later thought, but also
the continents of experience mapped in literature. A
good starting point for the more faith-based discussion
in the coming pages is that of our inner lives—or our
souls, in spiritual parlance. Good religion helps us to
cultivate and service our souls, with far-reaching consequences for our broader progress.

I have already voiced a firm belief that God is at work in many traditions, secular as well as religious.[2] That is a natural consequence of holding that all are made in the divine image. Exclusivist Christians who doubt this should consult their Bibles. In John 14:6, Jesus is recorded as saying 'I am the way and the truth and the life. No one comes to the Father except through me.' But the 'me' referred to here is none other than the Word of God who enlightens the hearts of all people, as the prologue to the fourth Gospel makes clear. So what is to be made of orthodox belief in the uniqueness and finality of Christ? An apparent contradiction is not insoluble. Christ is held to be unique in the sense that a new phase of human history was only made possible by his Passion and resurrection. So when Christians profess their faith in God the Trinity, they are acknowledging an irreplaceable given. But this faith also entails a confidence that all human beings possess a basic dignity, regardless of local differences, which renders the goal of universal reconciliation and a universal fellowship conceivable in the first place. Christians with concrete experience of interfaith dialogue regularly report that they have been changed by it: not that they have watered down their beliefs, but that their humanity has been enlarged through an encounter with the other. From this follows a no less robust sense that it is for God, and not anxious Christians, to judge how someone outside the visible Church is related to Jesus or has turned towards the Father.

With these points in mind, I quote with gratitude an insight expressed by Bertrand Russell in his autobiography, at a time when his lifelong antipathy to Christianity might have been softening: 'The loneliness of the human soul is unendurable; nothing can penetrate it except the highest intensity of the sort of love that religious teachers have preached; whatever does not spring from this motive is harmful, or at least useless'. This sentiment chimes with Christian teaching that we will eventually be judged according to the extent of our charity.

Such ideas in turn grow from the intimation that we are tenants in a house not of our own making, that our bodies are our 'lendings', in the expression used by King Lear in a moment of hard-won wisdom, and that therefore we are answerable to a truth we don't create. Our obliviousness of these points, especially in the developed world, feeds a reluctance to think about the inevitability of death. The historian and theologian Donald Nicholl never allowed his Christian identity to stop him from being enriched by non-Christians. To cite one example among many, he noted the astonishment felt by Tibetan Buddhists at what strikes them as a Western inability to confront the end of life. For by recalling this reality, we come to negotiate our time on earth with greater wisdom: to unpeel ourselves from selfish desires, for example, including what Iris Murdoch (herself sympathetic to Buddhism) called 'the anxious, avaricious, tentacles of self'. When we do this, according to many of the great religious traditions, we will achieve true clarity of mind.

The economist E. F. Schumacher, author of *Small is Beautiful*,[3] felt no clear spiritual leanings for much of his life. But in middle age he spent five weeks in a Buddhist monastery learning to be still, later reporting that the experience had changed him deeply. He realised that his

63

mental terrain had until then formed a constantly shift-
ing kaleidoscope of restless urges. According to the
Abrahamic faiths, it is also through silence that we move
forward spiritually. Nicholl records that the Hebrew
word for the presence of God, *Shekinah*, has the same
root as the Arabic word for the pause, or silence, that
Muslims observe at one point in their prostrations during prayer. This word is *Sukun*. 'So the Jew and the
Muslim are at one in the conviction that it is in silence,
in stillness, that God comes to dwell among men, to be
present to them and to transfigure them, as Jesus was
transfigured on Mount Tabor.'[4]

Sometimes the results of this will appear prosaic, at
least on the surface. When Rabi'a, the tenth-century
Muslim mystic, was approached by some of her followers in Baghdad and asked about the first step on the path
to virtue and patience, they expected a highfalutin pro-
nouncement. But she gave a two-word answer: 'Stop
complaining.' Initially taken aback, her hearers later
grasped that there was no point in talking of patience
until they had reined in the impulse to complain. In
short, they had begun to learn about detachment. As we
do too, our eyes can be opened to the critical difference
between reacting and responding. Our impulse is to
react spontaneously when we are offended in some way.
But if we are schooled in detachment, we will be able to
exercise freedom in challenging situations, rather than
behaving like other animals. Those who have advanced
along the religious path report that it is above all through
waiting on God in prayer—surrendering control and
beginning to know God as God through bodily as well as
mental disciplines—that we can grow in liberty of spirit.

Perhaps church teaching, soiled in many eyes by spent metaphors and other devaluations of the spiritual currency, can be refreshed against such a background. For the task of the grown-up Christian is to break out of the prison of the ego so as to attain an innocence at the far side of experience. Expressions of such innocence come in all shapes and sizes. When Nicholl was running one morning in the hills around Beit Jalla, near Bethlehem, he passed four Muslim labourers trudging up a path towards a quarry. One of these men thrust a handful of raisins into his hand as he passed, leaving Nicholl with a deep sense of thanksgiving. The man had performed an everyday act of kindness—albeit one resulting from many years of religious practice. Or take another, deeply tragic, example. In the unspeakable conditions of Auschwitz, Maximilian Kolbe, the Polish Franciscan, felt called to perform the ultimate sacrifice. A German commandant had just picked out ten Poles who were to be starved to death. One of them, Sergeant Franciszek Gajowniczek, on hearing his own name, broke down at the thought of never seeing his wife and children again. Fr Maximilian offered to take his place. By that act of self-sacrifice he not only put the seal on his own life, but also gave point to the strivings of all those beings through whom life had been transmitted to him over millions of years.

What effect does the gospel story have on those with ears to hear? Joy belongs at the heart of a Christian life, because the root meaning of the word gospel (*euangelion* in Greek) is good news. In his addresses to spiritual enquirers, no less a figure than Raniero Cantalamessa, preacher to the papal household, has regularly acknowledged the Church's responsibility for impeding a grasp of what the Good News amounts to. When Jesus announces in Mark 1:14–15 that 'The time is fulfilled, and the Kingdom of God is at hand; repent and believe the Gospel', we may be forgiven for associating the message more with gloom than with a mood of celebration. But this is partly because the Greek word *metanoeite* was wrongly rendered as *paenitemini* (and as *paenitentiam agite* in Acts 2:38)—do penance—in the Vulgate, for many centuries the main version of Scripture available to Western Christians. This poor translation survives. Erasmus, writing on the eve of the Reformation, was among the first European commentators to note that *metanoeite* really means 'change your mind'. In general, conversion in ancient Israel involved repentance and a return to the path from which one had strayed. But Jesus asks us to take a leap into the unknown, because salvation has already arrived. We have already glanced at the principle of justification in Chapter 2. Several other faiths prescribe what their adherents must do to obtain salvation. Christianity *starts* by proclaiming God's saving action—a message driven home by Jesus in narrative form, for example in the parable of the king hosting his son's wedding banquet, and inviting all and sundry regardless of rank (Matthew 22:1–14).

Why has Western Christianity often been associated with joylessness—and especially with negative attitudes to the body? Part of the answer lies with Augustine. Despite his colossal contribution to theology, psychology and wider culture, he overplayed his hand during the Pelagian controversy early in the fifth century by laying too much emphasis on the flaws in human nature. The imbalance was intensified a millennium later by Luther. Eastern Christianity does not discount the deep insight encapsulated by the doctrine of original sin. With its high view of the grandeur and dignity of men and women, however, Orthodoxy has been influenced far less by Augustine, and scarcely at all by Luther. A properly layered Christian model of the human person will balance the perspectives of East and West. Admittedly, our hearts sometimes turn to stone. We are prone to screwing up. God wills to implant a new spirit within us. But Catholics and Protestants alike have sometimes erred in seeing grace in negative terms—as a remedy for sin, not as a mark of the indwelling of the Holy Spirit.

The recovery of a theology of the Spirit in the West over recent decades can be ascribed to a mixture of influences, including the rise of the ecumenical movement and of Pentecostalism (the Christian counterpart to Islamic revivalism). Cantalamessa, well placed to observe this change, hails the picture of Christian life involved as 'joyous, contagious … with none of the gloomy pessimism that Nietzsche reproached it for'. Inhabit the narrative, and everything changes. The words of Ignatius of Litakia, a leading Syrian Christian, sum up a view held across the Christian spectrum:

Without the Holy Spirit:

God is far away,
Christ stays in the past,
the Gospel is a dead letter,
the Church is simply an organisation,
authority simply a matter of domination,

mission a matter of propaganda,
liturgy no more than an evocation,
Christian living a slave morality.

But with the Holy Spirit:

the cosmos is resurrected and groans with the birth-pangs of
the Kingdom,
the risen Christ is there,
the Gospel is the power of life,
the Church shows forth the life of the Trinity,
authority is a liberating service,
mission is a Pentecost,
the liturgy is both memorial and anticipation, human action
is deified.[5]

Life in the Spirit

Let us now revisit the account of Jesus's death given in
Chapter 2. I hinted there that some traditional ways of
interpreting this event are outmoded or mistaken. Jesus's
sacrifice does not represent payment of a ransom to the
devil, or appeasement of an angry deity. The more
coherent interpretation is that Calvary marked a fork in
the road of human history. God in Christ put himself at
the mercy of humanity, offering himself as the solution
to our ills and the fount of eternal life. God was spurned
and marked out for death, but accepted this rejection as
a way of remaining present to those who choose to
accept him. By raising Jesus from the dead, God revived
his offer of reconciliation and fulfilment.

I have already said that this book is not an advertise-
ment for a particular denomination. We can, however,
note a family resemblance in historical teaching on the

sacraments—rituals through which the community recognises a gift from God. They are held to apply the achievements of Jesus's ministry to the faithful. They are not injections of invisible fluid, but a spur to shaping the Christian's second nature towards union with God. Nature, when it responds freely to God's nature, can be said to be perfected by grace: one of the images favoured by Aquinas is of the ocean moving in more than natural ways through the influence of the sun and the moon.

Some readers may judge that a description of church teaching is one thing; an argument that Christianity is *true*—fundamental to our spiritual destiny, Good News, rather than merely good advice—quite another. The best practical counsel for seekers is that they should dip their toes in the water. Some testimony of Meghan O'Gieblyn, a contemporary American writer, is worth citing at this point. It is all the more germane because she repudiated the fundamentalist certainties in which she had been raised. At its best, she recalls,

> What made Church such a powerful experience for me as a child and a young adult was that it was the one place where my own thoughts and failings were recognised as accepted, where people referred to themselves affectionately as 'sinners', where it was taken for granted that the person standing in the pews beside you was morally fallible, but still you held hands and lifted your voice with hers as you worshipped in song … And it's precisely this acknowledgement of collective guilt that makes it possible for a community to observe the core virtues of the faith: mercy, forgiveness, grace.[6]

Part of the intellectual answer is that the Judeo-Christian tradition offers a richer, because truer, account of the human subject than does secular modernity. We have seen that philosophy often projects a model of modern man as free, independent, lonely, powerful, rational. He has heroic qualities, but is somewhat stunted spiritually. Note the contrast with Maximilian Kolbe, a saint rather than a hero: the difference lies at the heart of what I am trying to say. The hero is still the model held up by many contemporary societies. We sense that our task is to turn a given situation round, to make the story come right. Endless tales are told in which heroes stand at the centre. If the hero fails, disaster threatens. But as a Christian ethicist such as Sam Wells has observed, a saint can fail in a way that a hero cannot do, because the failure of a saint reveals the forgiveness and the new possibilities made in God, and the saint is just a small character in a story that is always fundamentally about God. 'So the saint's story is ... very different from the hero's story, and I think that distinction between saint and hero can portray the difference between philosophical ethics and theological ethics ...'[7]

An example from popular culture can clarify this. *Prison Break*, the Fox TV series, is a high-octane political thriller. Framed for a murder he didn't commit, Lincoln Burrows, brother of the protagonist, Michael Scofield, is sentenced to the electric chair. Michael sets out to spring Lincoln from jail. The plot entails outlandish feats of derring-do. Yet in the end, Michael triumphs not by living happily ever after (the usual destiny of the hero), but by giving his life to save that of his wife. What appears to be another prefabricated Hollywood drama is thus raised to another level. The legend on Michael's tombstone—'BE THE CHANGE THAT YOU WANT FOR THE WORLD'—recalls Mahatma Gandhi and points to the witness of a saintly character, rather than a merely heroic one.

Now look more closely at the shape of Meghan O'Gieblyn's practice cited above. Communal worship and private discipline of the kind she describes amount to something a good deal more robust than the wobbly structure delineated by a term such as 'spiritual but not religious'. Though not necessarily to be dismissed lightly—some people are put off church with good reason, of course—it is perhaps undeservedly popular all the same. Here's why. Sharper Christian commentators remind us that spirituality wasn't a word much heard before the 1960s. Since then, 'spiritual but not religious' has entrenched itself as a way of describing those who lay claim to the comfy feelings that can accompany religious belief, without having to get into the nitty-gritty or compromises of 'organised religion'. Spirituality should be about more than this. Rather than occupying a little department of our lives marked heightened emotions, it should involve a concerted journey towards God. This is why contrasting 'spiritual' and 'religious' amounts to a false dichotomy. Liberal Christians of an earlier generation unwittingly lent credence to this error by giving priority to private impulses. They thought that it is the horse of individual experience which pulls the cart of ecclesiastical structures. Many would now reverse this and say that it is the community represented by the Church which draws out and brings to fulfilment capacities that are latent within us. In other words, without community, 'spirituality' can become sentimental and inward-looking. Christians are thus taught to pray corporately as well as individually.

Contemplative prayer, whether practised alone or in company, has something in common with Eastern spiritual disciplines. The Buddhist picture of the world as at root an impersonal flux is not compatible with Christianity, but this does not mean that a monotheist cannot learn valuable lessons from Buddhism or other Eastern traditions. You allow your body to go limp and do your best to silence the wandering mind, breathe rhythmically, strive to let a riot of thoughts subside, especially those involving self-reproach and an often equally pernicious lust for self-vindication. Posture matters. Christians do not just kneel to pray in church because it is reverent, but because doing so can keep the upper body straight and the mind alert. The meditation stools in wide use are especially conducive to good physical alignment.

A common way of preparing the mind is through recitation of a mantra, which might be a phrase from the gospels, such as 'I am the bread of life' or (especially in the Eastern Churches) the Jesus Prayer: 'Lord Jesus Christ, Son of God, have mercy on me, a sinner.' Experts on prayer speak of how gentle repetition of a mantra, harnessed to simple loving will, can bring about a sense that the body is a receptacle or cave, so to say, where God's presence and action become gradually more apparent.

'Attending' to God should not involve thinking that we can picture him. A highly insightful writer on the subject warns that Christians are waiting on 'a Being that is beyond all thinking and beyond all picturing and therefore we do not try to think or picture, and whatever thoughts or pictures come into our mind we take absolutely no notice of them, we just reach out in love; peaceful, quiet and attentive.'[8] The source just quoted observes that we should not be expecting anything to happen on the surface, because the change afoot is believed to be more thoroughgoing. 'God is working deep in our soul. While we are in that quiet attentive state God is doing His work ... in the unconscious part of the soul, deep down in the spirit, so deep that our conscious mind is not able to grasp what is going on.'[9] Tradition associates this state with an awareness of an unbroken inner light. To vary the metaphor and put the point in explicitly Trinitarian terms, Christians believe that they can step into the stream of the divine life by holding fast to Christ and being supported by the Holy Spirit.

I hope that the rationale for such teaching will grow clearer during the course of this chapter. Now, though, it may suffice to underline another significant tenet: that contemplation should be a spur to action and not a substitute for it. William of Saint-Thierry, the twelfth-century Cistercian, suggested that love of the truth drives us from the world to God, and the truth of love sends us back from God to the world. Two centuries or so later, the Rhineland mystic Meister Eckhart enlarged on this insight by declaring that if you were in the seventh heaven of ecstasy and a poor man came to your door to ask for some soup, then the soup should be your first priority. Eckhart adds that a person performs an act of charity more effectively if he or she has first drawn close to God, the source of all truth.

What applies to contemplation is equally true of inter-cession. Petitionary prayer should not be confused with spiritual fantasies about manipulating the world. The process becomes meaningful when the petitioner has a personal stake in his or her prayer. I shouldn't pray for the hungry to be filled so that I will no longer be trou-bled by beggars; I should commit myself through some sort of giving to provide for the hungry. Likewise, those who pray for peace should pledge themselves to recon-ciliation in their own spheres. Some may infer from this that I am representing prayer as subjective—merely the source of a psychological boost. Not so. We do not need to accept occult ideas to see that intercession can have objective consequences. Take another example such as prayers for the coming of God's Kingdom. Since this process is believed to involve the free consent of human-kind, it is objectively strengthened when it is sought by Christians, especially when they pray as a body. So when members of a fellowship pray for some end, they are not trying to change God's mind about them, but to change their minds about God—to bring their wills into con-formity with his, and remove the obstacles standing in the way of his love.

Interpreting Scripture

Our saint–hero distinction drawn above also implies that a worldview like humanism may not shape up as well as many assume by comparison with Christianity. A confi-dence that secular resources provide everything requisite and necessary to a fulfilled life is the governing premise behind *The Good Book: A Secular Bible*,[10] the selection of

ancient and modern wisdom produced by the philosopher A. C. Grayling. His choices show his appreciation
for the classics of Greece and China especially; he also
draws on Romanticism, tying it in with the rationalist
tradition associated with Jeremy Bentham, Tom Paine
and Thomas Jefferson. Contributions from the Hebrew
Bible are excluded.

Grayling's project has merit as far as it goes (it should
go without saying that humanists can be much better
people than many Christians, as well as vice versa). But
The Good Book also rests on many of the mildewed assumptions we have already identified in New Atheist polemic,
especially that Scripture is little more than bad science
reflecting the stumbles of humankind yet in its infancy.
The real sense of the biblical narrative has been sketched
by a sociologist of religion such as David Martin, in a
major body of work extending over half a century. Rightly
understood, the Bible is an extraordinary and complex
human phenomenon, a library of books of every genre,
evolved over centuries and held together first in the
Hebrew Scriptures by one nation's quest for identity—its
account of what it means to experience God and be in
covenant with him—and then in the New Testament by
the ministry of an exceptional man believed by his followers to personify the Jewish nation. The informed Christian
can be as critical of young-earth creationist and other
fundamentalist interpretations of the Bible as any atheist
could wish. As we have noted, inspiration does not mean
dictation from on high.

The Old Testament starts with two pictures, one of a
creation recognised as good, and the other of the source

of a deep fracture which spearheads the search for atone-
ment and renewal. It leads to liberation from bondage,
which means both freedom of a people, and deliverance
from the self-centredness that is sin. It includes the rejection of idols, pictured both as images of the unknowable,
and the pursuit of wealth or power that we follow in
denial of our real duties towards God and neighbour.
Martin summarises the significance of the New Testament
as follows:

> [It is about God's presence with us] as flesh of our flesh, about
> the proclamation of an invisible kingdom and a banquet to
> which we are all invited, as well as about the signs of that
> kingdom and that banquet, about the absorption of … evil in
> the gift of body and spirit even unto death, the death of the
> cross, about healing of spiritual and physical wounds, the offer
> of a sign of peace, and the reconciliation of enmities, about
> rebirth, death to self and resurrection, and about the taking
> up of a redeemed humanity to share in the mutual exchanges
> of love which are the life of God.[11]

In other words this story, even though expressed in a
range of pre-scientific idioms, is central to everything
that inheres in being human. Martin's words provide a
potent answer to what have been termed the 'Kingsley
Amis' questions—what does this mean and why should
I care?—and the crass verdict on Scripture of Philip
Larkin, who said that the Bible is bilge. (His aphorisms
were nothing if not uneven.) In fairness, he was troubled
by the representation of God in the Old Testament as at
times despotic and vengeful. Among the difficult passages for a Christian reader are 1 Samuel 15, where Saul
is commanded to destroy the Amalekites, then censured

by God for showing mercy towards some of them, rather than blind obedience to the divine will. Or Exodus 32, where an orgy of violence follows God's command that the sons of Levi slaughter 3,000 of their own kin. But like many intelligent people who share his outlook, Larkin appeared never to advance beyond a literalistic reading of the text. I've already mentioned that mainstream Christianity has never viewed its Scriptures as the unmediated Word of God. The Church teaches that the gap between heaven and earth is only bridged definitively in the figure of Christ, and not in humanly authored accounts of his life, however inspired. And although the Old Testament was never disavowed by orthodox believers (not least because of the belief that Jesus was the Messiah of Jewish expectation), the New Testament nevertheless relativises earlier Scripture in important respects. Just think of how subversive the Sermon on the Mount would have seemed to many a pious Jewish ear.

A serious misinterpretation of the Bible is also evident in Steve Jones's book *The Serpent's Promise: The Bible Retold as Science*.[12] Jones, a geneticist, is another non-Christian (albeit less strident than Dawkins and Grayling) who has parachuted into theological territory without map or compass. His strategy involves juxtaposing reports of scientific facts with the supposedly mistaken attempts to account for natural phenomena given in Scripture. Story after story, book after book, are interpreted reductively. The prophets, for example, are represented as apparently having suffered migraine visions, explicable by science, rather than as launching a critique of injustice and idolatry, along with a concern for the well-being of all, especially the vulnerable, that would shape the Middle East and Europe for millennia to come.

Jones's weakness is philosophical as well as textual. He treats science and religion as separate spheres, respectively good and bad, rather than as evolving ways of interpreting our surroundings—and ourselves. Lost is any awareness that we do not merely investigate the natural world at a scientific level: we also seek to make sense of our lives via all sorts of evolutionary adaptations—agriculture, dance, literature—that have emerged from animal play, animal empathy, ritual and myth during a long history of tribal societies without much sense of the beyond, through supernatural king-god monarchies, to more recent societies with their religions of value transcending an awareness of the brute givens of existence.

In his illuminating study *The Meaning in the Miracles*,[13] Jeffrey John conveys a sense of the problems Christians themselves can have with biblical interpretation. John tells us that he had two Scripture teachers at school: Mr Davies, an old-fashioned Welsh Nonconformist who took the entire Bible literally; and Miss Tomkins, an Anglican with 'Modern Views'. If you questioned Moses's parting of the Red Sea in front of Mr Davies, an accusation of pride would follow in short order. Miss Tomkins explained the whole business in terms of tides and sandbanks. Both would have done well to heed the advice of Augustine 1,500 years beforehand to attend to the inner meaning of the stories concerned.

An episode such as the feeding of the 5,000 is misconstrued both by pious conservatives who only accept the text at face value, and by sceptics who simply assume that Jesus and the disciples shared their food, thereby encouraging others to follow suit. Like much of the gospel narrative, the story is fashioned to make a point—in this case that Jesus is the new Moses, because of the manna provided to the Israelites when they were hungry in the desert. A good commentary on the passage will also disclose that Jesus's actions echo those of Elisha, who provided miraculous sustenance to an army with a small amount of bread in 2 Kings 4. The evangelists are telling us that Jesus is the Messiah heralded by the Law and the Prophets, understood as the twin foundations of the Hebrew Bible. This distinctively Jewish presentation of Jesus continues with the feeding of the 4,000 a little later in Matthew and Mark. The different setting and frames of reference have been interpreted both as pointing to a two-phase process of mission (first to the Jews; then to the entire world), and to the institution of the Eucharist at the Last Supper.

Now consider another aspect of the first-century Palestinian thought world, namely the assumption that some people and groups were in thrall to demonic forces. We do not need to believe either in real devils with horns, or to dismiss reports of Jesus's exorcisms as relics of a now superseded cultural milieu, because biblical language about 'principalities and powers' refers to political entities, as well as to malign spiritual forces. And because of this, the healings Jesus performs often imply social liberation for a group, as well as for an individual. (This is plainly the implication of the cure of the woman with haemorrhages in a setting much exercised about ritual impurity.)

These comments can only scratch the surface of New Testament commentary. The gospels and epistles are among the richest texts in existence. But one unavoidable aspect of their interpretation centres on the connection between miracles and faith. Jesus's wonder-working appears to mark the arrival of a new and divinely ordained era. At the same time, this stands in tension with an emphasis on not relying too much on signs. When the Pharisees request one, Christ declines, telling them that they will only receive the sign of Jonah (Matthew 12:38–40)—in other words, the prophet's burial in the belly of a whale is being presented as a symbolic anticipation of the Passion and resurrection. In Mark's Gospel above all, Jesus enjoins the disciples to keep quiet about his miracles, an apparent anomaly long glossed as pointing us to an understanding of the true nature of messiahship. As generations of scholars have grasped, the disciples' commitment should not ultimately derive from the attractions of power. It may do to start with; then it must mature into an acceptance of the way of the cross.

The effect of this comes across with unparalleled sophistication in John's Gospel, especially after the risen Jesus has miraculously filled the disciples' nets in the Sea of Galilee. The Lord and his followers meet for breakfast cooked on a fire of coals, like the one at the high priest's home where Peter betrayed his friend thrice over. The risen Jesus then asks Peter three times whether he loves him, Peter answers yes each time, and Jesus in turn urges him to 'feed my sheep'. Peter's sin is expunged; the scope for reconciliation is revealed in all its richness.

The resurrection

For all its brevity, this chapter cannot avoid a topic as central as the resurrection. History and faith, the objective and the personal, are ineradicable features of orthodox belief. Jesus appeared to people whose confidence in him had crumbled, not to confident believers. It was the resurrection which created the Church and its faith, not the Church which created the resurrection. Those who see Christ's victory over death as only a metaphor can therefore be challenged on at least two grounds: not only that they risk circumscribing the power of God by laying down in advance what can and cannot happen, but that their supposedly rational understanding of Christian origins is in fact at odds with the historical evidence. The witness given by Christ's early followers is thus seen as the most credible explanation of all the available evidence.

This is an argument underlying the immensely painstaking work of New Testament scholars including Tom (N. T.) Wright in the English-speaking world,[14] and Stefan Alkier in Germany. These and other commentators have drawn attention to a cluster of linked arguments which make sense of the complex religious ecology of first-century Palestine. One, as we have noticed, is that Jesus's claim to speak for God, and even to embody God's purposes, would have shocked many mainstream Jews. Another is that the resurrection was seen by Jesus's followers as vindicating his claims. A third is that ideas about the resurrection held in the classical world were much more hard-headed than we might suppose.

A dramatist such as Aeschylus sums up a general classical view that people don't rise from the dead: 'Once a

81

man has died, and the dust has soaked up his blood, there is no resurrection' (*The Eumenides*). Belief in an afterlife had nevertheless developed little by little within Judaism. By Jesus's day, the Pharisees held that God's people would be raised to life at the end of time. But a range of belief was still evident. The Sadducees, for example, did not believe in the resurrection at all; other groups disagreed with the Pharisees over the form a possible afterlife might take. The Christian conviction that one person had been raised in advance of countless others was notable both for its novelty and for the scepticism that it prompted.

Though themselves Jewish, the first Christians broke with received opinion in other respects as well. It was no part of Jewish teaching that the Messiah would die and be raised to life. Wright has documented numerous other variations on traditional views—some exceptionally audacious—embraced in the early Christian community.[15] But if the resurrection had simply been invented sometime after Jesus's death, we should expect a far larger range of views, shading into disagreement, over what had happened to Jesus. (This only occurred with the rise of Gnosticism in the late second century.) In fact the gospels display a good deal of overall consistency, despite differences of detail, and an avoidance of imagery from the Old Testament deployed by other Jews who shared a belief in the resurrection. Again, if the gospel accounts were made up, it is more than likely that they would have made maximum use of traditional language and symbols, especially from the Book of Daniel. The distinctiveness of the New Testament is all the greater because the risen Jesus expounds the Scriptures on the way to Emmaus in Luke 22, but Luke does not tell us what the passages concerned were.

The highly important role of women, especially of Mary Magdalene, in witnessing to the empty tomb—even though the testimony of women was not accepted in legal settings at the time—has long been remarked on. Others note that while Matthew, Mark, Luke and John only view the resurrection as confirming Jesus's messianic status, Paul and the early Church Fathers see it as a curtain-raiser on the final destiny of the elect—in other words as central to the Christian message. This again suggests that the gospel accounts are not later accretions, but are rooted in an early oral tradition, free of detailed theological reflection and closer to the events they purport to describe.

The first Easter may look rather different with these pieces of context in mind. Mainstream Christianity affirms that the risen Christ's appearances were genuine. Sceptics have regularly written them off as hallucinations. Again, though, ancient observers were hardly less aware than we are that people's senses can deceive them. Traditionalist Christians can reply that 'hallucinations' could have been disproved with reference to Jesus's corpse, assuming it remained where it had been buried. They can add that Jesus's resurrection body—which can be touched, but also pass through doors—appears to subsist in both an earthly and otherworldly dimension. Andrew Davison, biochemist and theologian, speaks from the heart of tradition in describing the resurrection as overturning the natural order.[16] In that sense it can be compared to creation itself in its novelty. Neither event can be accounted for in terms of natural science.

The metaphysics of the resurrection clearly forms a vital hinge for Christian self-understanding. But the mere fact of the empty tomb is ambiguous, as are claims about the activities of the risen Lord. It should be emphasised that believing in the resurrection is not about bloodless intellectual assent to an apparently improbable event in the remote past. It entails the death of the old self and rebirth of the new that lie at the core of Christian proclamation. Just as baptism represents the drowning of the old self and the birth of the new, so does the resurrection, which is why Christian converts speak of their lives as a gift, and see the path of thanksgiving as the most appropriate way of affirming that Christ is risen.

The Trinity and eternal life

Another foundational belief is that Christ, though plainly a human being, was also God incarnate. I wrote earlier of Jesus's authority. On the other hand, we have also seen that his attention is constantly directed away from himself towards the God of Israel with whom he feels a level of intimacy that can only be expressed in radical terms. This was perhaps the hardest question faced by the early Church: how to describe a man who appeared utterly dependent and utterly free—who claimed a divine liberty and who was yet so obedient to God that you couldn't accuse him of trying to stand in the Father's place.

We also noted that side by side with the historical evidence stands the distinctive character of Christian worship. The prayer that Christians offer out of faith in God as Trinity is not a plea addressed from one agent to another, a movement from here to there. Instead, it involves contact with one who is both other and not other. The effect of Jesus's ministry was so momentous that it took centuries for the Church to reconceive its doctrine of God in response to a spiritual earthquake. Gradually there arose a conviction that God is not only initiative, but also self-giving response; that there is in God the generative or giving agency Christians term Father, and a responding agency called Son or Word, and that these two elements are equal. The teaching that Christ was 'of one substance' with the Father was not fully standardised until the fourth century. As suggested in Chapter 2, though, it had an empirical aspect rooted in spirituality. The apparently neater theory that God is a single, undifferentiated presence and Jesus merely his representative was rejected as unsatisfactory on two grounds. It didn't account either for Jesus's profound originality, or for the new vistas felt to have been opened up by the resurrection.

This awareness is of the highest importance. Judaism, Islam and some other faiths maintain that humanity has received a communication from God. The Church's claim, encapsulated above by David Martin, is more radical: that our destiny is communion with our Creator. Since the God worshipped by Christians is not a monad but an eternal exchange of love between the three divine persons, there is, so to say, space for us to be caught up in that exchange as adoptive children of God through grace.

The consolidation of belief in the Trinity was also a gradual process, but one that acquired its own logic. If we were to speak of God only as Father and Son, we would be led to picture a static reflection. Language about the Holy Spirit arises because of a need to say that there is more than just such mirroring in God. And it is because of this that a world can appear which may be drawn into the life of Father and Son. God, to reiterate an awareness underlying all other Christian proclamation, invites humanity to participate in his life. That is part of what the doctrine of the Holy Spirit represents. Scripture teaches that the mission of the Spirit is Christ's legacy to the world. The Spirit or wind of God is with us now, but the operation of this divine wind is left to chance. Without us, the wind is invisible. 'We are the leaves on the trees that show it up,' in the words of a poetically minded preacher I once heard. 'We are to swirl in the wind of Christ's passing.'

To gain a clearer understanding of immortality, we need to reacquaint ourselves with some of the Thomist categories described in Chapter 3. I have emphasised that Aquinas is resolutely anti-dualist. The relationship of the soul to the body should not be likened with that of the tea to the cup, say, but more to the connection between a smile and a face. We have seen that the soul is more credibly viewed not as a separate entity, but as the shape of a life, embracing the physical as well as the intellectual. The mistake made by a good deal of secular philosophy and Platonising religion is to suppose matter as such to be meaningless. By contrast, Aquinas makes clear that everything from digestion to having sex to making moral choices is saturated in meaning. Drawing in part on Paul's teaching in I Corinthians 15 about the resurrection of the body, developed orthodoxy teaches that God will give another carrier to the nexus of memories and beliefs that forms our earthly lives. Those who accept this teaching naturally cannot explain how it will unfold. Honesty entails an admission that the New Testament is ambiguous. The various footprints from intertestamental Jewish belief are there in the epistles—in the crudely physicalist doctrine set out in 1 Thessalonians 4; in the apparently dualistic model of 2 Corinthians 5; and in the blend of the two in 1 Corinthians 15. But it should also be noted that belief in eternal life is a function of convictions about God, and God's commitment to the human soul, rather than of theories that we possess an innate capacity to survive death.

Suffering, evil and universalism

A further unavoidable component of this outline is the problem of pain and suffering, usually known as theodicy. The challenge, never summed up in English more trenchantly than by David Hume (himself paraphrasing Epicurus), is stark. 'Is God willing to prevent evil, but not able? Then he is not omnipotent. Is he able, but not willing? Then he is malevolent. Is he both able and willing? Then whence cometh evil? Is he neither able nor willing? Then why call him God?' I do not believe that this deepest of conundrums for the believer can be fully or tidily resolved. Only the chronically insensitive suppose that the slave trade or the Holocaust or other colossal crimes can ever be retrospectively vindicated in some future settlement of spiritual accounts. Nor, for that matter, can the death from dysentery of a baby in Africa. Pain is not 'God's megaphone to the world', in the notorious expression—later taken back—of C. S. Lewis. There is in any case a limit to what can be achieved by rationalistic discourse: the ground on which the argument unfolds will always in the end be moral and practical. It can never be circumvented by following the path of logic and evidence alone. The resources of faith do not provide a demonstrative or even a probabilistic solution to the problem of the amount and degree of suffering in the world, but a resolve not to abandon a commitment to follow the way of love.

Yet thoughtful Christians cannot leave things hanging. One potentially fruitful way forward lies in revisiting a traditional model of God's standing in relation to the world. We have seen that classical Christianity does not picture God as a director—still less a puppet master—or (as deists and some Christians influenced by deism hold) that he has wound up a spring and retreated to let creation take care of itself. God is the unceasing presence holding everything in being at every given moment. He is not observing us from a distance, ruminating on whether or not to intervene. While activated by God, however, the world is different from him—hence our free will—and what is not God will by definition be subject to imperfection, decay, collision, conflict. Viewing monotheistic teaching in the round, we can infer that God's role is neither to cause tragedy nor to resolve it by our own canons of resolution. His relation to strife, rather, lies in the resources he offers for transfiguring it and taking it forward.

It is important to be clear about what this argument does and does not imply. Christianity does not support a naive confidence that things always happen for the best. Even when people turn hardship into a source of emotional and spiritual growth, this does not necessarily transform their suffering into an unmitigated good. Among those to have produced fruitful reflections on some of the darkest corners of human experience are Dietrich Bonhoeffer, the Lutheran pastor and theologian executed for his role in the bomb plot to assassinate Hitler, and Francis Tan Tiande, the Catholic priest from Canton in China who was sentenced to an indefinite period of hard labour by the Communist authorities in 1953, and did not regain his freedom for three decades. These great figures—and countless women and men like them—did not conclude that they were suffering for a reason. They judged that even the horror they faced could be opened to God. On this basis, Christians or Jews or Muslims looking back over a life marked by much strife can nevertheless conclude that it has all been drawn together by grace, rather than that their experiences are all vindicated or justified. They will be guided by hope rather than optimism. The big difference between the two is adroitly summarised by Jonathan Sacks:

> Optimism and hope are not the same. Optimism is the belief that the world is changing for the better; hope is the belief that, together, we can make the world better. Optimism is a passive virtue; hope an active one. It needs no courage to be an optimist, but it takes a great deal of courage to hope. The Hebrew Bible is not an optimistic book. It is, however, one of the great literatures of hope.[17]

In Christian eyes, the resources of God just alluded to were witnessed above all on Calvary—a revelation of what W. H. Vanstone has termed 'the limitlessness, the vulnerability and the precariousness of authentic love'.[18] Believing there to be an analogy between divine and human love, Christians can hold that the activity of God sets no limit on its own self-giving. From this springs a radical awareness: that divine 'superiority' in itself confers no moral right to respect. In particular, Vanstone warns, 'superiority of power confers no such right … [R]eligious imagery which displays and celebrates the supremacy of divine power neither convinces the head nor moves the heart.'[19]

God's work, rather, is laden with risk. As an outflowing of love, creation cannot be coerced still less predetermined, by the Creator. That things go adrift—sometimes tragically so—is not an indication that God has employed the wrong material, but that creation is genuinely other. Vanstone, a parish priest of great experience who pondered deeply and wrote very sparingly, deserves a careful hearing:

> If the creation is the work of love, its 'security' lies not in its conformity to some predetermined plan but in the unsparing love which will not abandon a single fragment of it, and man's assurance must be the assurance not that all that happens is determined by God's plan but that all that happens is encompassed by his love.[20]

These profound words argue against both the coherence and the morality of belief in eternal punishment. In defending the principle that God the creator of all is also saviour of all, David Bentley Hart agrees that it isn't possible to believe in God's goodness if God wills the perpetual torment of some. 'When we use words like good and just to name God, not as if they're mysteriously greater than when predicated of creatures, but instead as if they bear transparently opposite meanings, then we're saying nothing.'[21]

Hart—an Orthodox theologian, let it be noted—is on strong ground here, notwithstanding the number of figures down the centuries who have thought very differently about the meaning of hell. There are admittedly some ambiguous verses in the New Testament that appear to promise unending punishment for the wicked. But we have already established that plucking individual gobbets from Scripture like leaves off a bush is not the way to see an entire vista. Romans 5:18–19 and 1 Corinthians 15:22 are most representative of an underlying message in asserting a strict equivalence between what is lost in Adam and what is won in Christ. 1 Corinthians 15:28 confirms an understanding under which the Image of God (the Son or Word) comes to us, the broken image of the Image, in order that the image be restored. Equally resonant is St Gregory of Nyssa's vision in his treatise *De anima et resurrectione* of all spirits moving from outside the Temple walls in history, into the Temple precincts beyond history, and finally into the 'Sanctuary' of the divine presence, when God will be all in all.

5

SUPPLY LINES OF THE SPIRIT

The 'melancholy, long withdrawing roar' of religious faith, symbolised by the tide in Matthew Arnold's poem 'On Dover Beach', is of its time. Arnold's simile was especially ill-chosen, because tides turn. Equally wide of the mark have been forecasts of the imminent death of institutional Christianity, repeated *ad nauseam* throughout the twentieth century by communists, fascists, existentialists and later by any number of suppliants at postmodernism's gate. Three-quarters of humanity profess a religious faith; that figure is projected to reach the 80 per cent mark by 2050. The turnaround has much to do with the so-called third wave of democratisation during the 1970s, as well as smaller waves of freedom since then. In one society after another, politically liberated groups began to reject the secular shackles introduced by the first generation of modernising, post-independence leaders. The constraints had often been imposed from on high, both in the communist world and in countries including India,

Egypt and Turkey, where the elites equated secularism with progress. Today, where political systems reflect people's values, they usually reflect their deep religious convictions. China will be the world's largest Christian country within a few decades; it is now witnessing the mightiest religious revival in history. Spiritual conversion can trigger political change: millions of Chinese Christians are heralds of a more open society.

As I have reported elsewhere,[1] a record of faith-based political groups would include Vishwa Hindu Parishad in India (which sowed the seeds of Hindu nationalism reaped by the BJP during the 1990s), the Muslim Brotherhood in Egypt and Jordan, Hamas in the Palestinian territories, Hezbollah in Lebanon, the Hahdlatul Ulama in Indonesia, Pentecostals in Africa and Latin America, and, in the Catholic world, an array of forces including European Christian Democrats, Opus Dei, and the newer religious movements. Faith communities are also developing remarkable transnational capabilities, appealing to foreign governments and international bodies judged supportive of their aims. Whether one views these trends with relief or unease, a conclusion reached by two prominent American sociologists, Timothy Samuel Shah and Monica Duffy Toft, is fair:

> The belief that outbreaks of politicized religion are temporary detours on the road to secularization was plausible in 1976, 1986, or even 1996. Today, the argument is untenable. As a framework for explaining and predicting the course of global politics, secularism is increasingly unsound. God is winning in global politics. And modernization, democratization and globalization have only made him stronger.[2]

This is hardly to imply that Christians and others have any grounds for complacency. On the one hand, large patches of a country such as Britain can justly be described as post-Christian. Religious literacy is low. In place after place, redundant churches have been put to other uses. On the other, harmony between faith groups remains a remote goal in some parts of the world. Religious fundamentalisms are rightly described by the historian and novelist Lucy Beckett as 'shallow modern responses to shallow modern assumptions'.[3] The destabilising effects of fanaticism can be seen far from Syria, Iraq and Nigeria. Formerly secular challenges such as the confrontation between Israel and the Palestinians have taken on a more religious cast, while faith has stoked conflict from Sri Lanka to Chechnya to Sudan. Near the tenth parallel of latitude north of the equator, religious fervour and political unrest are reinforcing each other in societies from Nigeria to Indonesia. But given the persistence of religion, we can draw an obvious lesson for the time ahead: that if faith groups (especially the foremost global traditions: Christianity, Islam, Judaism, Hinduism, Buddhism and Sikhism) are not part of the solution, they will in all likelihood remain part of the problem. The question of whether and how other communities adapt to a changing world is clearly beyond the scope of this book. But I can reiterate that public Christian voices need to be self-critical as well as measured, and that the right tone of voice is best struck by drawing on theological resources rather than ignoring them.

In glossing the notion that religion embraces the whole of life, Christian thinkers have sometimes spoken of six dimensions to belief and practice: doctrine, ritual, myth, ethics, institutions and personal experience. Doctrine is necessary as a means of relating tradition to developing understandings of the world. This implies that the Christian way should involve a mixture of creativity and receptiveness. In other words, the community should aim at making professions of faith that are broad and inclusive, yet at the same time clearly deriving from what has been received from the past. Ritual is the main way of giving voice to faith in a religious setting; while myth, rightly understood, is the core underlying ritual. The great biblical narratives—culminating with Easter and Pentecost—will shape the outlook of the believer at both conscious and unconscious levels. Ethics naturally entails certain forms of behaviour, from decent conduct to at least an awareness of the self-giving love that has prompted greater feats of spiritual athleticism among the saints and countless others. Christians should have two priorities in particular, both essential if not always easy to balance: solidarity and social cohesion on the one hand, and a willingness to engage in a radical critique of society on the other.

If this sounds like hot air, look (to take but one example) at the evidence collated in a work such as Luke Bretherton's *Resurrecting Democracy: Faith, Citizenship, and the Politics of a Common Life*.[4] It is based on a four-year study of the groups London Citizens and Citizens UK, looking at ways in which community organising constitutes a form of democratic politics, bringing together people of different faiths and none to answer pressing social needs. Or—casting the net more widely—consider what a volume such as *Peacebuilding*[5] reveals about the Christian contribution to conflict resolution in scores of societies from Colombia to South Africa to the Philippines. In this light we can see the justice of Jonathan Sacks's description of religion as

> part of the ecology of freedom because it supports families, communities, charities, voluntary associations, active citizenship and concern for the common good. It is a key contributor to civil society, which is what holds us together without the coercive power of law. Without it, we will depend entirely on the State, and when that happens, we risk what J. L. Talmon called a totalitarian democracy, which is what revolutionary France eventually became.[6]

That many remain unconvinced by these claims is partly connected to secular liberalism's self-appointed role of referee rather than contestant in the public square. Acutely sensitive to the perceived imperialism of other worldviews, it tends to be coy about its own imperialism. Challenging a philosophy resting on complex clusters of assumptions is not easy, but one timely starting point might lie with Magna Carta. Eight centuries after it was promulgated 'for the honour of God and the exaltation of Holy Church and the reform of [the] realm', laws deriving from principles set out in this document secure freedom of belief across a vast belt of the world. Christians along with others hailing the theological dimension remind us that the two billion people who live in common-law polities are the document's heirs, and that almost every contemporary constitution has drawn inspiration from it. Magna Carta was biblically based. Stephen Langton, the Archbishop of Canterbury

who played a leading role in framing it, was a keen pro-
moter of ecclesiastical independence. But he was no less
keen to apply norms first set out in the Torah: that the
Israelites were not to be abused or enslaved, and were
themselves to do justly. At the heart of such a polity was
the administration of justice. 'You shall make for yourself judges and officers ... and they shall judge the people with just judgements. You shall not wrest judgement;
... neither take a gift' (see Deuteronomy 16:18–19). The
echo in clauses 39 and 40 of Magna Carta is clear:

> No free man will be taken or imprisoned or ... outlawed or
> exiled or in any way ruined nor shall we go or send against
> him save by the lawful judgement of his peers and by the law
> of the land. To no one shall we sell and to no one shall we
> deny or delay right or justice.

Magna Carta was reissued in 1216 as the Coronation
Charter of a new King, Henry III. Speaking at the
Church of England's General Synod in July 2014, the
theologian Nicholas Sagovsky pinpointed the link with the
covenantal theology developed by the biblical King Josiah:

> Just as with the covenant of the Hebrew Scriptures, which
> defined Israel as a covenant-people, so Magna Carta became
> woven into the self-understanding of the English nation. Just
> as the prophets of Israel recalled the people to fresh obser-
> vance of the covenant, so the constitutional thinkers and
> lawyers of the common-law tradition have refreshed and
> renewed our understanding of Magna Carta over 800 years.

Needless to say, the law in most Western societies does
not consider national life to be grounded in any particular religious text. In 2004, for example, many politicians

and civil servants resisted calls for a reference to God and the continent's Christian roots in the preamble to the EU Constitution. One clerical observer after another has pointed out that celebrations to mark the Magna Carta anniversary in 2015 rarely if ever mentioned divine law; we are therefore confronted with a tension between the enormous cultural footprint of Christianity on the one hand, and its concealment in a secular multicultural society such as Britain on the other. For evidence of a related situation in France, one could cite the writings of Pascal Bruckner or Alain Finkielkraut or Michel Houellebecq. They voice a sense that self-criticism in Europe has shaded into self-hatred. The nostalgia for past standards felt by conservatives is matched by a determination to wipe the slate clean on the part of their opponents.

Many who counsel a middle way hold that liberalism is not incompatible with the Judeo-Christian tradition, but, on the contrary, a legitimate development of it. Conservatives often ground their views on scepticism rooted in a sense of human imperfection. Yet liberals need not exclude this sort of awareness from their own calculations. When Richard Hooker locked horns with the Puritans during the late sixteenth century in support of a more open-handed form of Christianity, he did so out of a concern about Puritan hubris. Holding arguments from Scripture in tension with reason was based both on a sense of our dignity as children of God, and of our limitations. Hooker's descendants support a model of liberalism that sees politics as ordered towards peaceful co-existence and the preservation of the liberties of the individual within a pluralistic framework, rather than by a search for truth (religious or otherwise), perfection and unity. Such arguments are well elaborated by the philosopher Christopher Insole in *The Politics of Human Frailty*.[7]

Mainline Christians who embrace pluralism—liberal traditionalists, as it were—are not proposing that deeper commitments and aspirations should be swept aside to leave a relativistic blank slate. Preaching at his enthronement sermon at York a generation ago, John Habgood qualified his liberal impulses with a set of observations that are no less applicable in the twenty-first century. 'I am constantly surprised by what people *do* believe,' he noted:

> half-remembered bible stories, odd bits of science fiction, snippets of proverbial wisdom passed on through grandmothers or glossy magazines. There is evidence, too, of a huge and largely unrecognised reservoir of religious experience in all sorts of people who would be horrified to class themselves as religious. There seems to be a widespread diffuse awareness of some sort of religious reality, which can attach itself to whatever materials happen to be around.[8]

A society was liable to lose its bearings in the absence of focused awareness, 'a public frame, a shared faith, which can sharpen vague feelings into prayer and commitment and action', Habgood added, before immediately noting that many would think an archbishop presumptuous for saying so.

Negotiating between the Scylla of a free-for-all and the Charybdis of authoritarianism has rightly been called a lifetime's work. But I share a sense that there need be no final contradiction between a public framework of faith and a critical awareness of its limitations. One of the best attempts to ford these choppy waters in more recent times has come in Rowan Williams's distinction between good and bad models of secularism: the 'procedural' and the 'programmatic'.[9] Procedural secularism grants no special privileges to any particular religious grouping, but denies that faith is merely a matter of private conviction. Larger visions should be allowed to nourish the public conversation. Williams sees so-called programmatic secularism in a far less positive light, because it insists on a 'neutral' public arena and hives religion off into a purely private domain. Rather than resolving clashes of outlook, programmatic secularism risks inflaming social conflict by stoking resentment among faith groups. Williams's recipe for harmony is 'interactive pluralism', which encourages robust dialogue among faith communities and between them and the State. No one has received the whole truth 'as God sees it', so all have something to learn. Such an engagement is held to contrast with the subjectivity implied by multiculturalist attitudes: 'tolerance of diversity' can conceal a multitude of sins.

An inclusive Christian ethic will see cooperation with God's will as a nuanced business. It will involve empirical investigation, as well as reflection on time-honoured sources of wisdom. In the words of Nigel Biggar, a leading ethicist,

> the engagement between theologians and non-theologians on matters of public concern need not be any less fruitful or any less capable of reaching a measure of agreement than engagements between various types of non-theologians whose views

101

draw on conflicting convictions—say between communists and liberals … globalisers and ecologists, just war proponents and pacifists. The problem is not theology. The problem is not even metaphysics. The problem is that subscribers to world-views of all kinds—and no-one is not a subscriber—sometimes prefer to bully rather than to reason together.[10]

In cases such as abortion or assisted suicide, to cite two among many contentious matters, Christian and other campaigners will advance theologically based arguments about the sanctity of life, as well as practical arguments endorsed by many secularists. Religious voices will not and should not always get their way in a free society. They need to be held to account on the basis of coherence, viability and other criteria. At the same time, Christians cannot be expected to accept an interpretation of their beliefs that reduces them to the status of a buttress for secular morality.

There are many who do not want to censor religious voices, but assume nevertheless that the political advances of the past two centuries could just as well have been made through the deployment of secular reason. This view is far too hasty. The theological ingredient cannot be brushed aside. Take the feverish, often muddled debate on weapons of mass destruction (WMD) that unfolded before the Iraq war of 2003. Once you have identified a given public decision and described it, you may find it difficult to see how Christians could respond very differently from other people. But by that time, as the Evangelical theologian Oliver O'Donovan points out, the interesting part is all over. The identification and description of decisions are crucial tasks—tasks neglected by

George W. Bush and Tony Blair. Discussing the period before the invasion, O'Donovan poses and answers the following questions.[11] Why did WMDs become the sticking point with Iraq? Because of the UN Convention on WMDs. Why was there a UN Convention? Because of huge revulsion at the Western and Soviet policy of deterrence based on the threat of mutually assured destruction—a revulsion focused in considerable measure by the Churches. Why were the Churches interested? Because they had a longstanding, if partially eclipsed, tradition that asserted the need for discriminate conduct in warfare. What was the basis of this tradition? The belief that international conflict, though it lies outside the scope of human law, does not lie outside the scope of divine judgement, and that guilt and innocence therefore matter in war as well. (It is worth noting in this connection that Pope John Paul II, most Orthodox patriarchs, and virtually all other leaders of the mainstream Churches were united in condemning the invasion of Iraq.)

This example looks all the more relevant given the widespread tendency already noted to associate religion with violence. Common sense ought to tell us that religion is not a special case apart from other varieties of kinship bond: the romantic nationalism underlying so much conflict over the past century derives from ethnicity, history and linguistic differences, as well as from religion. Singling out faith-based motivation for acts of violence is irrational, because weapons are used in the name of an alleged greater good all the time. Islamist suicide bombers have learnt their deadly craft from secular exemplars. The roots of contemporary terrorism lie more in radical Western ideology, notably Leninism, than in religion. And in 1945, it was a secular liberal government in Washington which calculated that the destruction of Hiroshima and Nagasaki was justified for the sake of ending the Second World War and thereby averting an even greater loss of life. The incoherence of the saloon bar refrain that blames violent strife on religion is further demonstrated by the ease with which markers of identity become blurred. In Northern Ireland, to cite an obvious case, religion is deeply connected with the legacies of British imperialism and Irish nationalism. In other parts of the world, religious affiliations often shade into ethnic differences, which in turn merge with claims to land, water and oil.

Or consider the examples of the Balkans and the Caucasus, where religious loyalties can exacerbate ties which are fundamentally political. This subject cries out to be placed in the broader context of nineteenth-century and post-colonial nationalism. The imperial project of Russia from Peter the Great onwards—and especially Russia's conflict with the Ottoman Empire—brought waves of nationalism in south-east Europe and western Asia, frequently involving the redrawing of frontiers along ethnic or ethno-religious lines, population exchanges, and the subsequent persecution of minorities that were seen as not being truly Turkish or Bulgarian or Greek. Comparable processes later took place elsewhere, notably in India and Africa. We can thus find many examples of conflicts in which adherents of the same faith are enemies, just as, in other cases, two religions can be aligned. It is telling that Raymond Aron's classic study *Peace and War*[12] scarcely mentions religion at all.

Of course Christianity can sometimes go terribly wrong, however. Non-Muslims who see Islamism as uniquely menacing are probably overlooking deeply unsavoury elements in other faiths, including the identity politics inherent in Hindutva-based nationalism; the social authoritarianism seen on the Christian Right in the United States or in parts of the Eastern Orthodox world; and the militancy of some Sikh groups. Christians deployed colossal violence during the conquest of Latin America, while the glorification of death in battle (though also deriving from pagan antiquity) can be seen as a legacy of cultural Christianity in Europe. But the Churches have largely shed their triumphalist baggage since the Second World War, partly out of intense shame over the Holocaust. Sections of the Islamic world must now undergo an allied process, precisely through paying greater heed to major elements within Muslim theology. When Islam and Christianity are true to their guiding principles, both faiths insist on the dignity of the person as a spiritual seeker. From this should follow a recognition that freedom of belief is the first of human rights.

I have underlined the New Atheist tendency to single out religion for criticism in discussions of violence, while ignoring both blood-soaked atheistic regimes and the malignant exploitation of other bodies of knowledge such as science. If Richard Dawkins can so confidently distinguish between Nazi science and pure, genuine science, then Christians can do likewise in cases including that of Slobodan Milošević, the communist apparatchikturned-nationalist who issued a call to arms under the banner of Serbian Orthodoxy when it suited him after the disintegration of Yugoslavia.

Another common complaint, that Christianity is inimical to environmentalism, can also be questioned. Pope Francis's encyclical *Laudato si'*[13] makes clear that theological insights into the shape of a good society can be applied to debate on climate change. The broad consensus that the burning of fossil fuels could in due course bring about a disaster with millennia-long consequences is widely shared in the Churches. We are now also living in a new geological era, the 'anthropocene', in which human activity is affecting the planet's ecosystem profoundly. This has led to a complaint that the culprits are destroying the book of life before having had time to read it. Some environmentalists are plainly ambivalent about religion. But when Martin Rees, the Astronomer Royal, reflected on attending a Vatican conference devoted to sustainability, he was surely right to underline the long view that the major spiritual traditions can supply.[14] Each of the Abrahamic faiths has much to say about the value of frugality and deferred gratification; living for others includes making the sacrifices for future generations that richer societies are now being called on to implement. Church-sponsored reports on social matters have frequently been dismissed as naïve by commentators and politicians, especially on the Right. But what might once have appeared wishful has come to seem far-sighted. Maurice Strong, who died in 2015, was both a hard-headed businessman and chief organiser of the Earth Summit held in Rio de Janeiro in 1992. During the final decades of his life, he echoed Christian leaders across the globe in warning that affluent Western life-styles are not sustainable.

Though some have concentrated on God's granting of dominion over nature to humankind in Genesis, a reading of Scripture in the round makes clear that good stewardship is paramount. In *Ask the Beasts: Darwin and the God of Love*,[15] the feminist theologian Elizabeth Johnson ventures to see a parallel between the perspectives of Charles Darwin and many a Christian. Although Darwin's formal stance was agnostic, he developed a reverence for nature that could be termed religious. A Christian versed in science and theology will reject both the Gnostic views that disparage the material world, and the natural–supernatural distinction that divorces it from God's graciousness. This takes us a very long way from the matter-and-spirit dualism of Plato, Descartes and their followers, a point reflected in the *Exsultet*, a hymn of praise traditionally sung during the Easter Vigil.

In answer to a natural objection—that evolution entails great pain and struggle, as well as beauty—theologians have spoken of the 'deep incarnation' and 'deep resurrection' of Christ. John Paul II glossed the incarnation as 'the taking up into unity with Christ not only of human nature, but in this human nature, in a sense, of everything that is "flesh": the whole of humanity, the entire visible and material world.' This view is shared across the household of faith: St Paul describes the resurrection as entailing a promise that creation will be 'delivered from the bondage of corruption into the glorious liberty of the children of God' (Romans 8:21). That these visions are beheld by the eye of faith does not discredit them by definition.

Thoughts about the environment lead us to economics. Poverty has fallen at an unprecedented rate since the 1980s. This has much to do with economic liberalisation in India and China, where most of the world's poor still live. Progress on the Millennium Development Goals, relentlessly championed by the Churches and other groups, has been encouraging: two billion people were 'extremely poor' in 1990; in 2015, the figure was 836 million. Child mortality was halved during the same period; school enrolment in developing countries rose sharply.[16] Yet poverty and inequality remain scandalously high. In real purchasing power—not just money— someone living below the US poverty level, earning $11,000 a year, is in the top 15 per cent of the world income distribution. A person earning $28,000 a year, the median individual income in the US, ranks in the top 5 per cent. Someone on $52,000 or more is in the top 1 per cent. The bottom 20 per cent of the world's population earns less than $550 a year in US purchasing power, and lives in severe want. As Thomas Nagel and others argue,[17] these statistics suggest that most people living in rich countries are in a position to do substantial good for others at much less cost to themselves.

Some observers, a high proportion of Christians among them, blame inequality and other financial ills on capitalism. (It is sometimes quipped that half the Christian population generates the wealth that the other half can feel guilty about.) Theologians and preachers have long judged capitalism offensive because of Adam

Smith's nostrum that the consequences of an economic transaction cannot be deduced from its motive. An entrepreneur may enrich others indirectly by providing quality services, but his fundamental urge will in all likelihood be to enrich himself. This discussion calls for a clear head. The economist Paul Collier reminds us that one of the most important points of departure lies in asking why the poor are poor.[18] Certainly, poor people are regularly exploited by the rich: this was far more of a problem in the nineteenth century, but remains a significant menace in the sweatshops of the developing world. Generally, however, poor countries owe their poverty to an absence of the rule of law, proper tax collection and a modern capitalist infrastructure. In richer societies, *pace* Marx, workers are less susceptible to alienation because of incentives and other mechanisms that invest people with a sense of purpose.

This is hardly to let capitalism off the hook. In the financial sector especially, things clearly went ruinously adrift before the crash of 2008. The malaise had much to do with light-touch regulation and the thirst for a quick buck: asset-managers came to be rewarded more and more on the basis of short-term performance. Between the mid-1990s and 2015, the ratio of CEO pay to average pay rose from 20:1 to 231:1 in the US, leading to ills ranging from low investment to poor worker morale. The problem of a misalignment of private and social incentives is even greater. Collier's conclusion bears quoting:

> Smith's proposition that the market does a good job of aligning them, while true for many markets, is often seriously

wrong in financial markets. A gain made by one asset trader is matched by the loss borne by another. Such trade is not socially useless, but its social value bears little relation to the private returns. ... In Britain some of the brightest brains are diverted to the City from activities such as innovation, where the marginal social returns are far higher than the private returns, because innovations can be imitated. In their hearts, many of these people recognize that while enriching themselves they are not enriching society: they quit and do something more satisfying.[19]

Christian social teaching promotes the harnessing of market economics and social justice. Germany is a beacon in this respect: the reputation of a group such as Rhineland entrepreneurs stands high. We can grant that the European welfare state was largely made possible by private enterprise, and that governments should live within their means and be prudent with other people's money. At the same time, our rulers should also be vigilant about ills including monopolies and gross disparities in pay. Wealth creation is a general good, but unearned income is another matter. The undeserving rich are unlikely to be a positive force. And business cannot only concern itself with the interests of proprietors. It should also take responsibility for all other stakeholders: workers, clients, suppliers and the wider community.

Amid all the talk of re-equipping economics with a moral compass, the Christian contribution (especially, perhaps, the impressive body of reflection produced by the Catholic Church) is highly constructive. Its watchwords are the common good, trust, non-discrimination, the priority of the poor and disadvantaged, and stewardship. There is certainly a way to go before these principles become fully rooted, even in the Church. I have deplored the role of Christians in promoting discrimination on grounds of gender and sexuality, for instance, but have also made clear that theology contains the antidote to its own sexist and homophobic poison.

How should a wealthy person give in practice? William MacAskill's well-received book *Doing Good Better: Effective Altruism and a Radical New Way to Make a Difference*[20] is laden with good advice and information about the most productive charities. A notable strand in the debate centres on the value of utilitarian perspectives. Utilitarians tend to argue that it is wrong, for example, to spend $50,000 on training a guide dog for a blind person when the same sum might save the sight of 500 people in a developing country who are suffering from trachoma. Critics of utilitarianism lay more emphasis on local and personal aspects of reasoning. If I assume that the needs of everyone in the world are equal, this might cause me to downgrade my own projects and other causes that harness my energies.

The philosopher Peter Singer, author of *The Most Good You Can Do: How Effective Altruism Is Changing Ideas About Living Ethically*,[21] takes a utilitarian line, urging that the needs of the world's poorest trump the goods to which many better-off people devote their time. Christians are likely to sympathise, citing as corroboration the priority given by Jesus to the outcast and stranger. I understand this impulse, while feeling unsure whether utilitarians should have the last word. Other Christians might qualify Singer's view by maintaining that all kinds of goods can legitimately be aimed at, even if they are not always maximally beneficial. Suppose that Mary and John are both highly altruistic people, and both believe in God. Mary trains as a nurse and goes to work among the poor in India. John, judging that he can fund a whole team of nurses in both India and Africa if he earns a large salary and gives much of it away, opts instead for a career in business. John's decision is indeed highly admirable. Viewed *sub specie aeternitatis* though, it is not self-evidently superior to Mary's. When the great New Testament scholar and musician Albert Schweitzer decided to cut short his distinguished career in Germany to become a doctor and missionary in Gabon, west central Africa, he was partly motivated by spiritual imperatives not captured in the utilitarian net. In brief, he wanted to save his own soul, as well as those of others. A Christian ethic should balance utilitarian and non-utilitarian perspectives. It is rich enough to accommodate both.

* * *

The British among others are renowned for a focus on the here and now. George Orwell famously described his compatriots as a nation of 'stamp-collectors, pigeon-fanciers, amateur carpenters, coupon-snippers, darts-players, crossword-puzzle fans'. Yet an interest in harmless pursuits shouldn't stop people from lifting their eyes to the hills as well. It seems to me especially important to think about transcendent commitments in a society based on individual rights and the pursuit of happiness. Our culture finds it easy to talk about instrumental goods—the right to work, to privacy, to be treated decently—but harder to confront deeper questions involving truth and purpose. Secular thought is not so firmly grounded that it can afford to dispense with Christian sources of wisdom; if we write off our history, we risk writing off our future as well. This seems all the truer in an era when the hobbies of a more innocent age have given way to the mixed blessings of technology. Left-wing and conservative thinkers alike warn that the Internet only enriches those who have already become rich through reading serious books. Long before the digital revolution, a wide range of figures were voicing concern about the young and not so young people who scorn the past. Those who do so display what has been termed an 'ethnocentrism of the present' that is no less narrow-minded than old-style jingoism. Other contemporary idols—especially materialistic consumerism—deserve to be dethroned. The key to both our individual and social flowering lies in Jesus's new commandment: 'Love one another; even as I have loved you' (John 13:34).

If you have made it to the end of this book and your inner jury is still out, then you have my gratitude for at least giving me a hearing. If the body of belief I have explored has left you less sceptical than before, then taste and see more of the many richer forms of sustenance available. Since I am conscious of offering nothing in these pages that I have not received, it seems right to end another chapter with the words of someone else—Samuel Taylor Coleridge in this case—whose insights have an abiding lustre. Like many in a tradition stretching from Paul to Augustine, Dante and Pascal, Coleridge judges that the heart of our humanity lies in a twin awareness: of our disfiguration on the one hand, and our capacity to conceive and body forth transfiguration on the other. Our station in life is irrelevant, he continues. For as long as our hearts listen, we have the means to recognise in Christianity 'the substantiating principle of all true wisdom, the satisfactory solution of all the contradictions of human nature, of the whole riddle of the world'.[22]

NOTES

1. FOG IN A CRAGGY LANDSCAPE

1. Frank Skinner, *Church Times*, 19 August 2011.
2. Anthony Green, *Private Passions*, BBC Radio 3, 30 November 2014.
3. Bryan Appleyard, *The Sunday Times*, 2 November 2014.
4. Brian Cox, *Start the Week*, BBC Radio 4, 14 March 2011.
5. Iain McGilchrist, *The Master and His Emissary: The Divided Brain and the Making of the Western World* (Yale University Press, 2009).
6. Richard Dawkins, *The God Delusion* (Black Swan, 2006).
7. Marilynne Robinson, *Absence of Mind: The Dispelling of Inwardness from the Modern Myth of the Self* (Yale University Press, 2010).
8. Sam Harris, *The End of Faith: Religion, Terror and the Future of Reason* (Free Press, 2006).
9. Daniel Dennett, *Breaking the Spell: Religion as a Natural Phenomenon* (Penguin, 2006).
10. Christopher Hitchens, *God Is Not Great: How Religion Poisons Everything* (Atlantic, 2007).
11. Antony Flew with Roy Abraham Varghese, *There Is a God: How the World's Most Notorious Atheist Changed His Mind* (HarperOne, 2007).
12. I am grateful to Professor Albert Weale of University College London for recounting this anecdote to me.

13. Edward Feser, *The Last Superstition: A Refutation of the New Atheism* (St Augustine's Press, 2008).

14. Thomas Nagel, *Mind and Cosmos: Why the Materialist Neo-Darwinian Conception of Nature is Almost Certainly False* (Oxford University Press, 2012).

15. Jerry Coyne, *Faith vs Fact: Why Science and Religion are Incompatible* (Viking, 2015).

16. David Bentley Hart, *Atheist Delusions: The Christian Revolution and Its Fashionable Enemies* (Yale University Press, 2009).

17. David Bentley Hart, *The Experience of God: Being, Consciousness, Bliss* (Yale University Press, 2013).

18. Alister McGrath, *The Dawkins Delusion? Atheist Fundamentalism and the Denial of the Divine* (SPCK, 2007).

19. John Polkinghorne, *Science and Christian Belief: Theological Reflections of a Bottom-Up Thinker* (SPCK, 1994).

20. John Polkinghorne, *Science and Religion in Quest of Truth* (Yale University Press, 2011).

21. Janet Martin Soskice, *The Kindness of God: Metaphor, Gender, and Religious Language* (Oxford University Press, 2008).

22. Keith Ward, *The God Conclusion: God and the Western Philosophical Tradition* (DLT, 2009).

23. Francis Spufford, *Unapologetic: Why, Despite Everything, Christianity Can Still Make Surprising Emotional Sense* (Faber, 2012).

24. See www.the-brights.net (last accessed 13 January 2016).

25. Dawkins, *The God Delusion*, pp. 180ff. For a ruthless dissection of Dawkins's view see, for example, Bentley Hart, *The Experience of God*, p. 333–4, n. 1.

26. Timothy McDermott, *How to Read Aquinas* (Granta, 2007), p. 29.

27. Ibid.

28. Karen Armstrong, *Fields of Blood: Religion and the History of Violence* (Knopf, 2014).

2. RESETTING THE COMPASS

1. For a highly insightful account of this terrain, see, for example, John Cottingham, *The Spiritual Dimension: Religion, Philosophy and Human Value* (Cambridge University Press, 2005).

2. For an overview of this subject, see Tom McLeish, *Faith and Wisdom in Science* (Oxford University Press, 2014).

3. Bentley Hart, *Atheist Delusions*, p. 97.

4. Lawrence Krauss, *A Universe from Nothing: Why There is Something Rather than Nothing* (Simon and Schuster, 2012).

5. Roger Scruton, *Gentle Regrets: Thoughts From a Life* (Continuum, 2005).

6. Ibid., pp. 226–7.

7. Roger Scruton, *The Spectator*, 31 May 2014.

8. For a more detailed discussion of this train of thought, see Rupert Shortt, *Rowan Williams: An Introduction* (DLT, 2003), pp. 73–80.

9. *Alpha News*, November 2004–February 2005, pp. 20–1 (see also www.alpha.org).

10. Alan Isler, *Clerical Errors* (Jonathan Cape, 2001).

11. Colm Tóibín, *The Testament of Mary* (Penguin, 2012).

12. Philip Pullman, *The Good Man Jesus and the Scoundrel Christ* (Canongate, 2010).

13. Herbert McCabe, *God Matters* (Geoffrey Chapman, 1987), p. 93.

14. See, for example, René Girard, *Violence and the Sacred* (Johns Hopkins University Press, 1977).

15. Nicholas Mosley, *Experience and Religion: A Lay Essay in Theology* (Hodder and Stoughton, 1965).

16. Ibid., p. 156.

3. GOD IS NO THING, BUT NOT NOTHING

1. Cited in Christopher J. Insole, *The Realist Hope: A Critique of*

Anti-Realist Approaches in Contemporary Philosophical Theology (Ashgate, 2006), p. 166.

2. John Habgood wrote an account of the event in *The Independent* on 4 May 1992.

3. The Hebrew Bible does not speak with one voice on this subject. Genesis 2, however, is normally cited as implying that man does not consist of a separate body and soul, but is 'a living *nephesh*', that is, 'a living unified being'.

4. McDermott, *How to Read Aquinas* (Granta, 2007), p. 54.

5. Ibid., pp. 4–5.

6. St Thomas Aquinas, *Summa Theologiae* (*ST*), 1a 2ae 91.1–3.

7. Aquinas, *ST*, I.2.3.

8. Dawkins, *The God Delusion*, pp. 100–103.

9. Aquinas, *ST*, 1.46.2.

10. St Thomas Aquinas, *Summa Contra Gentiles*, 1.16.3.

11. For a very lucid account of this subject, see Edward Feser, *Aquinas* (Oneworld, 2009), Chapter 3.

12. Peter Atkins, *On Being: A Scientist's Exploration of the Great Questions of Existence* (Oxford University Press, 2011), p. 17.

13. Denys Turner, *Thomas Aquinas: A Portrait* (Yale University Press, 2012), p. 142. The passage comes from Chapter 4 of Turner's book, 'God', which gives an exceptional exposition, at once clear and profound, of Thomas's philosophical theology.

14. Victor Stenger, *God: The Failed Hypothesis* (Prometheus, 2007).

15. Roy Abraham Varghese, Appendix A, 'The "New Atheism": A Critical Appraisal of Dawkins, Dennett, Wolpert, Harris and Stenger', in Flew and Varghese, *There Is a God*, p. 167.

16. Michael W. Tkacz, 'Aquinas vs. Intelligent Design', at http://www.catholic.com/magazine/articles/aquinas-vs-intelligent-design (last accessed 13 January 2016).

17. Stephen Jay Gould: *Wonderful Life: The Burgess Shale and the Nature of History* (Norton, 1989).

18. See, for example, Simon Conway Morris, *Life's Solution: Inevitable Humans in a Lonely Universe* (Cambridge University Press, 2003).

19. John Polkinghorne, 'The Trinity and Scientific Reality', in J. B. Stump and Alan G. Padgett (eds), *The Blackwell Companion to Science and Christianity* (Blackwell, 2012), p. 534.

20. John Haught, *God and the New Atheism: A Critical Response to Dawkins, Harris, and Hitchens* (Westminster John Knox Press, 2008), p. 107.

21. Polkinghorne, 'The Trinity and Scientific Reality', pp. 527–8.

22. Rupert Shortt (ed.), *God's Advocates: Christian Thinkers in Conversation* (DLT, 2005), pp. 55–60.

23. John Cottingham, 'Descartes and Darwin' in *Proceedings of the Aristotelian Society Supplementary Volume*, vol. 87, issue 1 (2013), p. 274.

24. Coyne, *Faith vs Fact*, p. 184.

25. Dawkins, *The God Delusion*, p. 137.

26. Ibid., pp. 137–8.

27. Gideon Rosen, *The Times Literary Supplement*, 31 May 2013, reviewing Nagel, *Mind and Cosmos*.

28. Immanuel Kant, *Prolegomena* 352.

29. John Cottingham, *Philosophy of Religion: Towards a More Humane Approach* (Cambridge University Press, 2014), p. 35ff.

30. Paul K. Moser, *The Evidence for God: Religious Knowledge Reexamined* (Cambridge University Press, 2009).

31. Rupert Shortt, *Rowan's Rule: The Biography of the Archbishop* (Hodder and Stoughton, 2014), p. 14.

4. A FAITH OBSERVED

1. See McGilchrist, *The Master and his Emissary*, Chapter 12.

2. For many Christians, the key text in this regard is *Nostra Aetate*, the Second Vatican Council's 'Declaration on the Relation of

the Church with Non-Christian Religions', 28 October 1965 (www.vatican.va).

3. E. F. Schumacher, *Small is Beautiful: A Study of Economics as if People Mattered* (Vintage, 1993).

4. Donald Nicholl, *Holiness* (Darton, Longman and Todd, 1981), pp. 6–7.

5. Ignatius of Litakia, discourse given at the Third World Assembly of Churches, July 1968, and published in *The Uppsala Report* (Geneva, 1969), p. 298.

6. Meghan O'Gieblyn's article originally appeared in *The Point Magazine*. It was reprinted in *The Guardian* on 26 November 2014 as 'How do you sell God in the 21st century? More heaven, less hell', available online at http://www.theguardian.com/news/2014/nov/26/-sp-my-life-in-hell (last accessed 13 January 2016).

7. Shortt, *God's Advocates*, p. 180.

8. Fr Matthew ODC, *Contemplative Meditation* (CTS, 1979), p. 15.

9. Ibid., pp. 15–19.

10. A. C. Grayling, *The Good Book: A Secular Bible* (Bloomsbury, 2011).

11. David Martin, *The Times Literary Supplement*, 3 June 2011.

12. Steve Jones, *The Serpent's Promise: The Bible Retold as Science* (Little, Brown, 2013).

13. Jeffrey John, *The Meaning in the Miracles* (Eerdmans, 2001).

14. See, among an immense body of work, N. T. Wright, *The Resurrection of the Son of God* (SPCK, 2003).

15. For summary treatment of this very intricate area of study, see the record of Wright's dialogue with Flew in Appendix B of Flew and Varghese, *There Is a God.*

16. Andrew Davison, *Times Literary Supplement*, 18 September 2015.

17. Jonathan Sacks, *To Heal a Fractured World* (Continuum, 2005), p. 166.

18. W. H. Vanstone, *Love's Endeavour, Love's Expense: The Response of Being to the Love of God* (DLT, 1977), p. 57.

19. Ibid., pp. 61–2.

20. Ibid., p. 66.

21. David Bentley Hart, 'Is Hell Forever? Universalism and creation', video available online at https://www.youtube.com/watch?v=3dOsKzh7Kyw (last accessed 13 January 2016).

5. SUPPLY LINES OF THE SPIRIT

1. Rupert Shortt, *Christianophobia: A Faith Under Attack* (Rider, 2012), Introduction.

2. Timothy Samuel Shah and Monica Duffy Toft, 'Why God Is Winning', *Foreign Policy*, 9 June 2006, available online at http://foreignpolicy.com/2009/10/19/why-god-is-winning/ (last accessed 13 January 2016).

3. Lucy Beckett, *Times Literary Supplement*, 27 November 2015.

4. Luke Bretherton, *Resurrecting Democracy: Faith, Citizenship, and the Politics of a Common Life* (Cambridge University Press, 2014).

5. Robert J. Schreiter, R. Scott Appleby and Gerard F. Powers (eds), *Peacebuilding: Catholic Theology, Ethics, and Praxis* (Orbis, 2010).

6. Jonathan Sacks, *The Times*, 3 February 2010.

7. Christopher Insole, *The Politics of Human Frailty: A Theological Defence of Political Liberalism* (University of Notre Dame Press, 2004).

8. John Habgood, *Confessions of a Conservative Liberal* (SPCK, 1988), p. 8.

9. Rowan Williams, *Faith in the Public Square* (Bloomsbury Continuum, 2012).

10. Nigel Biggar, '"God" in Public Reason', *Studies in Christian Ethics* vol. 19, no. 1 (2006), pp. 17–18.

11. Shortt, *God's Advocates*, Chapter 14.

12. Raymond Aron, *Peace and War: A Theory of International Relations* (Transaction, 2003).

13. Pope Francis, *Laudato si': On care for our common home* (CTS, 2015).

14. Martin Rees, *The Times*, 15 August 2015.

15. Elizabeth A. Johnson, *Ask the Beasts: Darwin and the God of love* (Bloomsbury Continuum, 2014).

16. *The Guardian*, 25 September 2015.

17. Thomas Nagel, *Times Literary Supplement*, 20 November 2015.

18. Paul Collier, *Times Literary Supplement*, 25 September 2015.

19. Ibid.

20. William MacAskill, *Doing Good Better: Effective Altruism and a Radical New Way to Make a Difference* (Guardian Faber, 2015).

21. Peter Singer, *The Most Good You Can Do: How Effective Altruism is Changing Ideas About Living Ethically* (Yale University Press, 2015).

22. Samuel Taylor Coleridge, *The Friend* (Princeton University Press, 1969), p. 524.

INDEX

INDEX

INDEX

INDEX

INDEX